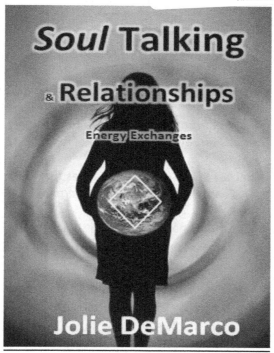

TABLE OF CONTENTS

Preface-pg.2

Introduction-pg.4

Everything is intermingled; What is the definition of a soul?

What *is* Soul Talking?
The relevancy of Soul Talking
How I learned to Soul Talk

Why relationships can be draining. The No Regret Rule

MINI CHAPTERS

Chapter 1: Everything is energy-The Basics-pg. 10

Chapter 2: About the Shift in the Earth and Universe-pg.11

Chapter 3: 10 Things you should know-pg.118

Chapter 4: Cord cutting-attachments and clearing your aura.
What's an Aura? What are Chakras?-pg. 42

Chapter 5: Interesting Stuff- that "matters"
Fear be gone- no regret rule-pg.64

Chapter 6: What the heck is a thought form?
Inner talk Bad teacher vs. Superhuman-pg.84

Chapter 7: Soul Talking™ techniques; How to Soul talk with you,
How to Soul talk with others
Ya Feel it!-pg.88

Chapter 8: Entitlement or Energy Exchange?-pg.111

Chapter 9: Empathic abilities-pg.117

Chapter 10: Energy Exchanges with Angels & Spirits/Universes
and Parallel Exchanges-pg.125

Chapter 11: Are we a "Good Match or Soul mates?
Techniques of How to Manifest with Equal Energy Exchange
Love/Relationships, Job, Tangible stuff, Knowledge and Self-
realization and Money-pg.131

Chapter 12: Success stories-pg.158

Preface by Sabrina Bennardo, LCSW.

Sabrina Bennardo, LCSW, is a licensed psychotherapist and relationship expert with more than 18 years of counseling experience including private practice in New York and Florida.

"The Soul Talking Technique ™ is effective in healing relationships. It's amazing that one can feel the energy change within and become balanced – I recommend the technique to my clients and have personally experienced the positive shift."

The Soul Talking Technique ™ provides a way to exchange positive energy that clears the relational space between people.

Often single men and women see me because they are distraught over not being able to forgive or let go of a past love that has moved on. I have met some who choose to remain in resentment for over 20 years, keeping themselves in their own prison. They swallow a bitter pill of resentment with every thought, and anger expressed about the partner they feel scorned them. This is poison to their soul. The Soul Talking Technique ™ is a powerful way to let go of the resentment and bring forgiveness into their soul; resulting in peace and allowing for the space to attract a new love relationship.

I believe Jolie to be the best clairvoyant. She truly is a "Messenger of the Light." I trust her guidance to the utmost degree. When she recommended I use The Soul Talking Technique™ with my father, I experienced an incredible shift in our relationship. In fact, after not speaking for some time, I received a beautiful message from him on my birthday right after I did "Soul Talking." After personally having that amazing experience, I started sharing it with my clients and continue to do so. I'm thrilled to have this technique as one of my power tools to offer and it is a joy for me to see their relationships and lives shift as a result.

This book will allow you to have a new way to create a positive shift in your relationships causing a positive shift in your life. Read on and enjoy Jolie's gift of sharing her messages. She is a blessing to know and a gift to us all. I'm lucky to have her in my backyard. I'm excited for you to have this opportunity to experience her and her messages. Also, to find out how to clear negative relationships energetically and peacefully, enabling you to create the life you desire.

Sabrina Bennardo –LCSW Licensed psychotherapist and relationship expert, Heart Connection Center Boca Raton, FL.

Soul Talking
& Relationships

Introduction by Jolie DeMarco
Everything is intermingled

Did you know that everything that exists is "energy"?

That means you are made up of vibrations and frequencies. That includes your pet, your furniture and that tree outside your house. Everything is energy. Energy consists of positive, negative and null vibrations which carry frequencies. Yep. It's true. That is simple science. Everything is intermingled because everything that exists is energy.

Intermingled? Yes. Our energy vibrations touch each other and intermingle a lot. Just like when we meet someone and have that thought of *"hmm, they are cute."* No physical touching needed to intermingle energy because that *"they are cute "*was a positive thought vibration that emits out into the atmosphere as a frequency. Get it? I'll get into that much deeper as you read on. You need to understand how energy exchanges affect you and all existence. But you really need to know some basics first.

Our commonalities

We all have souls and we all have relationships. We all are souls that live together on Earth. Some relationships are great, some suck, some need releasing and some relationships just need mending.

What is the definition of a Soul?

A soul is the infinite energy of you. Not the skin and bones- but the energetic part of you. I can describe a soul in many ways, but I want you to try to visualize a beautiful crystal clear diamond that is the size of a basketball. Notice the clarity in this rather large diamond. Picture this as your soul's energy so you can imagine it tangibly.

Every relationship we have or had- and any or all patterns we adapt or create from our lives is inside this diamond. As life happens, we have good and bad relationships. We also learn behaviors good, bad and neutral. During our lives our clear diamond gets some blemishes from the negative occurrences or actions we chose or were involved in. Now our shiny clear diamond isn't so clear anymore. Soul talking helps you clear up those blemishes that tarnished your shiny diamond energy- that is your soul. We want that shiny diamond to be grade A -close to flawless, clear and brilliant. The clear diamonds are brilliant and attract brightness. Everyone loves shiny bright things. Soul talking can brighten your precious diamond soul. This analogy is one way to understand the concept, but it gets much more interesting.

What is a Soul talk?

There are *two ways* to Soul talk. Number one is performing the soul talk with you. This is the human you talking to the soul of you- the diamond within. The second way to soul talk is with your soul and another person's soul.

When you soul talk- you can replace the negative of anything such as negative thoughts, negative habits, negative behaviors- including addictive behaviors. This process can be done to help you advance in your life and help you make positive or equal exchanges with yourself and other people that you have negative energy blemishes from. Soul talking is an energetic exchange of negative to be positive or equal between your soul and another soul. When you perform the soul talking technique- ya literally feel it!

More examples of what the Soul Talking technique™ can help you *let go* & release:

- Allowing others to treat you badly.
- Releasing jealousy, resentment and manipulative behaviors
- Fears; of loneliness, fear of success-self sabotaging your own success
-Releasing the feeling that you are unworthy of love or good things in life
-Releasing the addictions of drugs, overeating and negative habits
-Realize and release submissive behaviors

Soul talking can help you place *positive vibes* to replace negative thoughts and habits. Soul talking is done without confrontation because it is an energy exchange-which means it is an energy meditation. Yes, you heard me. It is done energetically.

This is how it works

Soul talking allows the self-the soul energy of you and your human body & mind achieve positive energy. For example: something that you have passion for, it could also be a goal. You are replacing negative emotions and thoughts that vibrate at a low frequency with a higher positive frequency that will make you happier and healthier.

 Your inner strength is YOU allowing YOU to basically accept and give yourself permission to move forward and let go of whatever you want to!
 However, if you really don't want to- you won't.
 Your soul is the pure energy of you.
 Your soul is your higher self, the all knowing you.

The human part of you can advise the soul to let go or erase or add whatever *you intend* with *thoughts and actions*.

Intention is what you desire and project. Knowing the meaning of the word can help you understand how to feel it. Sometimes we hear words but really don't understand the true meanings; this will help you. There is a step by step version of how to Soul talk later in this book. You can read the detailed directions especially for you.

Who wrote this?
How I learned to soul talk

My name is Jolie DeMarco- most people call me a messenger of the light. There's no coincidence that you found me or this book. In guiding over 6,693 people in the last 8 years with private spiritual counseling sessions, there has been one repetitive issue. Yes, you guessed it- mainly of relationship issues or what I call *differences.*

These differences can be from one's perception. A person's perception can be learned and or effected by their environment, family, religion, values, health or habits. It derives from one's overall actions of what they know to be their "normal," and their understanding of the words they use. Interesting enough, I asked 300 people what their definition of love meant to them. What a variety I got back.
There is no right or wrong- just different as I mentioned.

In the last 10 years, I have been listening to the voices in my head- and luckily enough, those voices have been accurate about 85% of the time. Now, that's my normal 'cause I'm clairaudient.
I had to learn how to ask those "voices" for the correct information! I learned that communication is the key and listening to their source of knowledge had many answers for me.

Once I established how to ask information for me- I learned how to ask information for other people. When I listened, I heard and learned *correctly.* All was great and I wrote this book of the teachings. The explanations were astounding. **Soul Talking and the no regret rules were the start of this new evolution of mending people and their relationships resulting in positive emotions and outcomes.**

How is this relevant to Soul talking and relationships?

Well, since I am able to connect with Angels, spirits and universal energies *they* wanted to send *me* messages and *knowledge* to share with "other humans." I gracefully accepted.
Plus, I had some of my own stuff to mend.

Chapter 1

Everything is Energy-The Basics

Our world is a relationship mecca. I share very important skills of how you can have positive and equal relationships with everything. Including those people you have had negative outcomes with. I explain *how everyone* in the world can make positive "energy exchanges." I was also taught new ways to manifest what we want- bringing positive results. My ultimate energy exchange is sharing these techniques with all of you. You will learn how energy "works" with your body on an energetic level and with other people.
And get this! You can do it without confrontation!

I describe easy ways for you to communicate with energy frequencies of the soul. I know these tips and step by step meditations will advance your true existence. You will feel complete in your life.
You don't have to be into metaphysical stuff to understand these techniques. It is for everyone all lifestyles and all belief systems to utilize and simple to follow.

I show you how to cleanse your aura. I include energetic ways to let go of negative attachments and clear your soul's energy from negative patterns. All of this knowledge is taught with *the Soul talking and energy exchange* techniques.
Let's get to it. First let me inform you about *Shifts on Earth -and how they are relevant to energy exchanges-*

Chapter 2

About the Shift in the Earth and Universe

Here's the story:
Since there are cosmic occurrences that can change the atmosphere – and these changes affect the energy around the Earth- these changes affect us.
 I am saying the Earth's vibrations can change. It's true -ask NASA!
When there are atmospheric changes - we can feel changes on Earth.
For example: if a meteorite comes close to the Earth- it can change the vibrations around the Earth. In turn - this can change lots of things on Earth. For one - it can shift our energies, our human aura's. These shifts and changes are energetic. They are energetic vibrations that can reach our auras vibrations and shift us. All in all –everything- everyone can be affected.

Here is another example of a vibrational shift in the Earth:
When there is a full moon. Lots of us feel differently on a full moon. We can feel a bit happier, some people may be sad-and some people feel unruly.

We know the moon affects humans because our human body consists of mostly water- approximately 80%. Remember the old wives tales of fisherman proving that catching fish is due to the tides? This relates to the moon's energy? Yep.

"The gravitational pull of the moon and the sun creates tides on the Earth. While tides are most commonly associated with oceans and large bodies of water, gravity creates tides in the atmosphere and even the lithosphere (the surface of the Earth). The tidal bulge that occurs during high tide in the world ocean follows the revolution of the moon, and the Earth rotates eastward through the bulge once every 24 hours and 50 minutes. The water of the entire world ocean is pulled by the moon's gravity." This paragraph included facts according to the website About.com/geography.com.

If you look at it this way- our bodies are mini oceans affected by the atmosphere.

Cha... Cha- Changes...

Among many changes, I believe that in the future- telepathic skills of "listening and receiving" will be one predominant way of communicating with each other. The term I use is called *"tele-talking."* Tele-talking is telepathically connecting a human mind to another human mind using similar vibrations and frequencies. I believe people will be able to additionally communicate with other energies that exist. This will be a cool new way that enables us to converse- watch out cell phone companies!

Respect

The energy exchange is treating each other with respect. This is to exist equally with all energies on Earth and beyond.

With all of the new changes in life, respecting all that exists enables us to comprehend that vibrations affect us all. Learning new ways to attract what we want and need. Understanding vibrations and frequencies is just a part of moving forward. What I find most interesting-is *how to* use all of this positive information in our everyday lives.

Manifesting is one form of exchangeable communication. We all can be masters of manifesting! If we use this energy properly we can live better and be balanced.

It seems only fair to be happy, loving and kind to ourselves and to others.

Balance

On a bigger scale- knowing *our world* can affect other existences sounds crazy! This *unknown* that may exist- is mind boggling. I am assuming humans and other forms of life are sharing the same atmosphere.

If all of us are of higher vibration -which means happy- our atmosphere and all that is in it -makes a better place to reside. This includes humans to other humans on Earth.

 If we have an even or a balanced energy exchange with these other far-way places or worlds- including our Earth- we all would be much better off in general. And speaking about our planet Earth-we really need to work on our relationships here. People can change their energy –they/we can change it to positive.

Think about it. Because as I see it- right now-what *we* are currently doing is *not* an even energy exchange with our own Earth. Obviously, it's not working out too well. Ya know with global warming, contaminated water, chemically altered food and all that.

I want an even or positive energy exchange with everyone, everything and all existence.

I listened to the guidance of these "spirits of the light.' I realized their knowledge about *new ways* of maintaining and advancing on Earth will bring infinite positive exchanges.

I hope you can realize that it all makes sense. Be open- like me -and then you can "listen too." These guides explain: "*Every energy exchange counts!*"

"Let Life Flow- Let the universe guide you in infinite ways of happiness."

-Jolie DeMarco

Knowing yourself

Knowing *you* is the first step in understanding other people. I call it feeling fulfilled or balanced. If you feel *un*fulfilled, that is the *only reason you need* to move forward and change that feeling to be filled. I also say this *is* the first step to self-realization.

What are some ways that help you with this?

Start by making lists. Get a paper and pen and sit in a relaxing place without distractions. To be clear, I want you to make a list of what you like now versus what you liked 2 years ago.

You will make a few lists. One for example will be just for personal goals or wants at this time in your life, then do a list for work/career or a job. Then take another sheet of paper and write what you like and don't about your current relationship with significant other, If you don't have one yet, make a list of what you would want of them. You can make lists of relationships with family, friends, lovers, and relationship with *yourself*. **Here are a few examples**:

This list is of work.	This is a list of a significant relationship
Like vs. Dislikes	**Like vs. Dislikes**
I like being around people I hate talking on the phone	I love going out to dinner with my significant other I hate when they text during dinner

You get it. Of course you really want to get detailed and do at least 6 of each subject or more. This gives you clarity and insight about your current life. If you need to makes changes or set goals, this listing inspires you to do that. Moving towards your positive personal path is the goal, along with self-realization of what goals you have inspired to reach.

You don't have to have a PHD. To *see* the cycles of life, you just have to *acknowledge* them.

Trust me; your self-realization comes fast with these tools in the next chapters. Read on to release negative, replace with positive and bring advancement to your lives and your relationships.

Everything is "Energy"

Everything is energy. You are energy. A tree is energy. Even a rock -has incredible energy.

Once you understand how energy works it's easy to realize the healing effects on people, things and you.

Our human bodies need to have high vibrational energies within and around us to heal and maintain on all levels. These levels are physical, mental, emotional and spiritual. These combined make us whole and balanced- and keep us feeling well.

Every day - we can pick up energies from objects, places and other people. Each of us produces and emits energy vibrations.

 This includes energy of our thoughts. Thoughts are vibrational energy too! *Thoughts* are vibrations and our *physical voices* are vibrations that carry various frequencies. Some of your thoughts or verbal words may or may not be of high frequency. High frequency carries positive energy.

Thoughts we create are considered *thought forms*. Thoughts can be positive or negative or null. If your thought is negative, the energy goes out as negative energy. Negative means lower vibrations. If that thought is about you and *is negative* -we call that a *"self –sabotage energy thought form."* These can do harm when they are a constant in a person's aura.

If these negative vibrations are not cleared out of the aura in reasonable time they can cause damage. They can cause damage by allowing illnesses as physical symptoms and/or unbalanced emotions- as well as mental stress.

Before I get into the nitty gritty details of auras, cord cutting, chakras and all that jazz- I would like you to first read these basics to help you get in touch with your inner self. Remember it is all intermingled.

Chapter 3

10 THINGS YOU SHOULD KNOW

WHEN EXPLORING YOUR INTUITION

Have you been thinking a lot lately or have you received some "signs" to start exploring your intuitive senses? Most of us come to a point where we ask or want to ask someone—anyone—how does it work? What exactly is intuition? Do I have it? Does everyone have it? Can I control it? There are so many questions regarding this beautiful, mysterious part of your life (and the beyond). Intuition can be described in many ways, but I believe it is trusting and knowing the inner part of "you."

My mission is to make sure everyone can have the tools they need to help them in preparation for the shifts in life. Let's face it, the unknown can be scary. I've had several occasions where I thought I might be crazy or thought I was talking to myself inside my head. As I said-I was!

Sometimes I felt as if I was taking on emotions of everyone around me, which I later found out was my ability for psychic empathy. Understanding basic information about your intuition through guidance of exploring yourself is very important.

I wrote this chapter because when I first started exploring my intuition, I had so many questions. I attended many spiritual classes and read countless books to discover this specific information. Hopefully, I am saving you a lot of time and money by writing what I've learned.

If I could have had this bit of information lumped all into one source, I would've been further ahead on my life journey. I would have advanced much sooner in learning and understanding about the spiritual world. Now I am sharing **10 basic things you should know when exploring your intuition**.

"An open Mind has infinite possibilities"

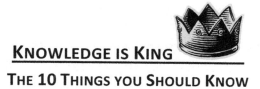

KNOWLEDGE IS KING
THE 10 THINGS YOU SHOULD KNOW

1 INTENTION

This is the *most important* to me and should be to all of us. Intention is the thought, the visualization to really mean what you are saying, thinking, feeling or doing with all your heart and soul.

Simply put, **Intention is what you desire and project** during your work, prayers, light work, healing or intuitive readings, and just every day in your life. While doing whatever it is you are doing or thinking, add "intention"; care about what you are doing, emotionally; "feel" what you are doing or thinking. That is what I call Intention.

Why is intention important aside from helping to make you a better person? Because it's important to have good intentions when connecting to your source so that your outcomes are positive. Intention is the key to reaching your intuition and spiritual explorations

I hope you are only giving love, light or both to your intentions—keeping the "light" in your work or thoughts.

I apply Intentions to all I do, and ask anyone if they can tell the difference in my work when I don't. It is amazing how Intention—this positive emotional high vibrational energy—can change your life and others for the better.

Energy, we are all energy—all made of vibrations which are energy. Think of music, the vibrations you hear are energy waves that we can't see, but feel and hear. We all have different energies. Some of us are soft, light, and comfy. Some of us are louder, bolder, stronger. It doesn't matter. If the intentions of whatever you are doing or placing the intention on are good, no matter what your energy is, it is high vibration. When an intention is good, good is from the light and light is high vibration.

Good intentions are high vibrations. If you are an energy sucker—a vampire as some say—your intentions may not be in the light, and probably not on purpose. However, once you are mindful you realize that everyone can connect to their source. When I say "source" I'm talking about positive energy, mother Earth, and/or your god. You can channel this energy from the light source without taking from others. Reiki is a modality of this teaching or energy healing. There are several modalities you may research and learn.
Let's talk about sensing energies.

Do you know how you can walk up to someone and instantly know that they are in a bad mood or spewing negative? Immediately your body tends to move away from this person because you feel their energy field, which is a low vibration. It doesn't mean they will always be of low vibration; it is just you sensing that person's negative emotions in their energy field at that particular time. When a person is truly happy they are of higher vibrations and, of course, when they are unhappy the energy surrounding them can be of lower vibration.

You want high vibration energy, which begins with good, loving Intention.

Actions without intentions are mindless actions. Make what you do -count in a positive way.

Understand if there is "no thought" there is neither positive nor negative intent which is a null- there was nothing behind your action or thought.

2 ASKING

Asking is one of the most effective ways of manifesting your loving thoughts or affirmations. It sounds too easy, and yes, it actually is easy!

When you ask the universe and state precisely what you are asking for (as long as it is in loving ways with good Intention) you are placing that good energy out to the universes and spirit world, and yes, also yourself. This becomes an affirmation or prayer. This is positive programming for you and the universes to hear the vibrations so that *the ask* or request can be heard and acknowledged.

When asking, make sure your Intention is for the greater good of all involved, be truthful and honest about what you are asking, and don't forget to visualize the outcome as it has already come true. I always finish my asking of the universe with a "thank you" and blessing. But a "thank you" will suffice, being grateful for the actions to be manifested helps tremendously.

For example:
If you are currently in poor health, you may ask, "Universe, I am asking to be healthy on all levels, physically, mentally emotionally and spiritually." "I am asking specifically for my knee, specifically for my left knee to be in perfect working order for full range of motion of my left knee." You will be asking with loving intention and visualize yourself well. You can picture yourself running on the beach, your knee is well and you, as a whole, are feeling well and your body is working perfectly!

Ok I know this ask sounds wordy, but, the more detailed information or specific information you state and the more you visualize the outcome, the better the message can be understood.

Think of it this way, if you were hearing a rumor, it probably has passed through several people before you heard it. Do you think it was as accurate as when it first started? Probably not. As this rumor passes through many storytellers, the story changes a bit here and there. It's kind of like a fishing story. Somehow as the story goes on, the fish becomes bigger and bigger depending who is telling the story, or the catch more difficult. I think you get what I'm going for here. There's another very important message here: Make sure your Intentions are true! Use only positive wording or you will get what you ask for without knowing you asked for it!

Here's an example of what **<u>NOT</u>** to do. This ask is using negative connotation:

"Dear universe can I have a rich man to meet, but **not** with bad health or small house , I want him to be good and **not** mean."

This is an incorrect way of asking. You are using negative connotation by using "**not**". Spirit guides and others in the spirit world do not hear negative connotations well, so they hear that you want a rich man with bad health or small house. State what you want from a positive point of view.

Use positive, loving intentions and your mind can be very a powerful thing.

When asking the universe you should state your ask with positivity in both directions. In other words, ask for your future husband to be respectful to you and that you'll be respectful to him; this creates a balance of energies, this creates a "positive energy exchange." Here is that same scenario asked correctly:

"Please, I ask the universe for this with loving intentions. I am and I allow myself to meet and marry an attractive man who is abundant in money, is in good health, has healthy habits, owns a nice home, is caring, respectful and has a wonderful sense of humor. I am and I allow myself to be respectful to him, I also am attracted to him and we have similar sense of humor and we are happy together in a loving relationship. Thank you. I am grateful."

Remember to be confident in asking and make sure you keep feeling that the intention is true. I often hear clients say, "I said the positive affirmation" and I always follow up with asking them, "Did you mean it? When you said your affirmation, did you feel it?" I also ask them: Did you think that you deserve what you asked for? As you asked and after you finished asking?" Most of the time a client will say, "No, I didn't feel like I truly deserved what I was asking for." I can't tell you how much it means for you to place the true intention and feeling it-You have to believe in what you're asking for. Be confident. Everyone deserves good things!

There *is also another part* of asking you need to understand, other than affirmations, there is the mystery voice or noise.

Let's say, for example, that you sort of "hear" things and you are not sure if they are coming from you, in your head, or they are from an outside source. The first thing you should do is ask, "Are you from the light"? Immediately the "voice "should say "yes." If "no" or you hear nothing then please refer to the Protection section below immediately! If "yes," then that is great.

If you are at the point of your intuitive exploration where

you can hear, then it's very important to ask the "voice" who they are and what their intentions are. Are they from the light, spirit guides, angels?

Now ask, "What is your name?" If they don't give you a name, be patient, maybe they want you to name them so you can identify with them by what makes you comfortable. Ask if they are here for a specific purpose, to help you maybe become a healer, to teach you, or to help you with some lesson you might have to learn.

At this this point, receiving a name is not important as you know you have spiritual contact with either your higher self, or an angel, spirit, spirit guide or loved one from the light. So be thrilled and happy!

Now, I have come across several people who have outside sources they discovered that are not their higher-self speaking to them and, by the way, have been yelling at them! The most likely reason these people are being yelled at by these spirits is that the spirits are feeling ignored. Once you have asked and confirmed that a spirit is from the light, and then you can ask them to please stop yelling because you can hear them now and are going to listen to what guidance they have for you. If you are a person that just hears "noise" it may be several spirits talking at once, maybe hundreds! This means you have to ask them to only speak one at a time, after all, you are only human!

I had one client whose guide was yelling so loud she had gotten headaches. I reviewed the whole process of "asking" with my client and told her to ask her guide if her guide was female because my client told me she had a female voice. I suggested that she ask the guide nicely (always be courteous and nice, you wouldn't speak to anyone if they were rude) to please, if she could create an accent, like an English accent, so she could distinguish her guide from her own thoughts. It worked! Her guide was so nice and accommodating she started expressing with an English accent to help my client. They now have a great relationship!

All in all, don't be afraid to ask and communicate truthfully with your guides or visitors from the light. They are guides; they want to give you "guidance". They are here to show you positive options only and because you are of free will you can always make your own decision—always. If you don't "hear" per say a spirit or guide, you may "feel" their presence. This feeling can be warm, or an indication of positive vibrations, in your presence. If you find that the spirit who you view as a guide is telling you what to do with your life in a demanding or negative way, or if you get a bad energy feeling around you, please go directly to the "Protection" section later in this chapter and read it, and re-read it! Remember, if this spirit or the energy of that spirit, contacting you feels negative then protect yourself and don't communicate with them.

Now you are communicating with the Light energies, this is great!

Here's an exercise you can use to practice, and can be done alone or with a group.

Asking the Universe

This is a session where a group works together with visualizations, by "Asking the Universe" for what we need or want for ourselves or another. You can do this exercise with just yourself or a group, both are very powerful.

First, we say the following words together and afterwards, each person will take a turn to state a request to the universe as if it has already been manifested. After which, all as a group (or you can) "imagine or picture" that request for the person who asked the universe. Approximately one minute each.

In the steps below, state #1 through #4 together as a group, then each person will make their request at step 5. Once everyone has made their requests and visualized the request, the group will say #6 and #7 together with loving intentions. You can do this alone if you don't have a group. Of course group visualization would be more powerful, but even alone it is extremely powerful.

Say Together:

1. We come here today to ask the universe for guidance.
2. We ask with only loving intentions to manifest our requests.

3. We are powerful, loving and strong. We wish only the best for all those involved in our requests and for the greater good of all involved.
4. We are always safe and surrounded by Love.
5. Each person, individually, makes their request.
   After each person's request we say together:

6. The Universe has heard your request_____ (person's name) and is fulfilling your needs for the greater good of all involved.

   After we all have asked the universe for our request we say together:

7. We are grateful. Thank you, Universe, for the loving energy you send our way. We have projected powerful, loving affirmations as a group by visualizing in Loving Light and manifested these requests to be true and realized. Positive energy surrounds us and the universe. We understand the universe will hear our requests and fulfill them as they are powerful, positive and loving.
8. **Manifesting for you: "life" as you want it is best.** Be detailed in what you want and positive vibration in how you think or say these with intentions(true feelings) that you want, and deserve these things or people in your life with   an   equal"   energy   exchange"

   Example:
9. *I am and allow myself* (this wording avoids self-sabotage) to marry a man that has healthy habits, he is (physically, sexually and mentally) attracted to me and I to him, he is

intelligent, humorous, is abundant in money, he loves me as much as I love him, we are monogamous to each other, he believes in me and I in him, we are compatible and happy together. We trust each other, we are monogamous and only to each other. I deserve this in my life now, this year (example: say the month, day and year including our Earth   dimension)

10. You can add or delete what you wish but only use high vibration words, and remember even a thought is energy and can manifest or negate what you desire. So after you say this affirmation, Please know and think and say that you deserve it and you deserve each other, otherwise a simple thought such as you in your head saying" well, if it happens," THAT just negated it! This energy went out to the   universe   as   null   or   nugatory. "Believe it and know it-"everyone deserves good things in life, including you!

3 Accepting

Allow yourself to believe there is more out there beyond human life forms. This is important.

Accepting the information you receive from your guide without freaking yourself out is a big plus. You must learn to allow yourself to accept help from others; it doesn't make you weak, it makes you stronger. This is not as easy as it sounds. Learning to accept the information you receive requires trust. Sometimes accepting in general is hard for many people.

I like to give the following example because there are a lot of people out there that are "givers", as I like to say. When you are always giving that is nice; it makes you feel great! So why do "givers" have such a hard time accepting? We all know a friend, or maybe this is you, who refuses a gift or favor by saying, "No, no I'm good, please take it back." By not accepting the gift or gesture that person who didn't accept or say thank you just took the feeling of "goodness" from the giver. I'm sure you know what giving feels like; it feels really good, but by not accepting the gesture you just denied that person the positive emotion. That's not nice! What the givers have to realize is that it makes others feel good to give too. So, accept! Givers also have to realize the *difference between accepting and taking*. There is a huge difference! If you are *being offered, it is not taking*! Please, *all you givers learn to accept* as well. It makes others feel good. This was also explained by the guides in the "energy exchange" messages.

I have one more example:

Let's say you are the go-to person at work. Some of your co-workers ask you to do things for them all the time, almost on a weekly basis. You know those tasks are really part of their job, but you are too nice to say "no," and you really don't want more work anyway.

Here is a Hypothetical situation:
Let's use the name Jim. Jim is one co-worker that always asks you do to some of *his paper* work and- you do it. Then

Monday, you are out on a personal day, and your boss asks Jim to do a report. The boss is waiting in Jims office specifically for that report- ya know the ones you always do for him...Jim is out of luck today. The boss asks Jim how come he cannot do the report he asked him for. Jim tells the boss man that *you* usually do it for him. The boss says: "but that's your job- Jim." Jim replies yes, sir. I know I am sorry. Big boss man says: "Jim, you're fired."

My point is that you enabled Jim, but you could've empowered him. Here is how. When Jim asked you to do his reports, you could say, Jim I would love to, but I have a lot of work to finish. I do have a few minutes to show you how to do them. Then take time to show him how. If Jim was full of it and was passing the buck, he'll just say oh,, no thanks. If Jim was sincere- Jim would take the time to learn from you- *that's you giving empowerment.* I do realize sometimes it is faster to do a report for him than show him how- but *if you really want to genuinely help a person, you teach and share.*

 A good mantra *"I am always learning and I will always share."*

4 Trusting

Trusting is about yourself and your true feelings—your intuitiveness. Just trust. Leave your doubts and insecurities at the door and see how much stronger you are, but remember to only be stronger in loving ways with good loving intentions for all involved, including the universes.

Trusting your source and *yourself* will help you understand this whole "communication" or contact from the other dimensions thing. Even if you decide all this information is not for you, that's cool. Please still learn to trust yourself. That little voice or feeling you have to go right instead of left, just try it, listen and do, see if it brings you goodness. Trusting yourself is one of the most beautiful things you can do for yourself. It brings confidence in all you do. Practice trusting you.

5 Sacred Space

A sacred space or place is important because it makes you feel safe and helps you tap into your psychic intuition comfortably. I believe that if we all had our own little sacred place, we would all be much less stressed in today's world. Find a place in your home, outside, or even at a beach or park. Go to this place at least a few times a week or when you feel you really need some "me" time. Use this location to meditate and release any feelings that are not positive. You also can use this place to ask the universe, renew your energy, and recite your affirmations and gratitude to others and your loving beliefs.

Having a sacred space is amazing. It can be in your home or your yard, it could be the beach or anywhere that you feel safe, comfortable and can relax. Once you have found this space, big or small (my friend's sacred space is in the closet so the kids can't find her), make this space yours by adding some little things like a few gemstones or a picture of a vacation place that made you feel "Zen". This is a space that you know you can go to and just breathe. If you decide to start contacting your guides or asking the universe for anything you can be sure this is a good place where you can place good intentions to do so.

Some people like to make their "space" like an altar, placing flowers for themselves and their guides, lighting candles, misting some essential oils, burning incense. It's all good as long as you feel good there. This is your "happy place". If you have a good imagination or visualization skills you can always bring your sacred place with you by using your mind to visualize and bring it to wherever you go. I actually do this a lot.

6. Clearing

Everyone has heard of clearing space, right? Not cleaning, but clearing. But it is kind of similar. Clearing your space means energetically cleaning auric debris from the electromagnetic field or the aura and other energies that surround your body. The space can be the space surrounding your body, your home, work or whatever space you occupy. Clearing helps you stay balanced physically, mentally, emotionally, spiritually, and will help you receive messages clearer.

You can clear by sage-ing or using your good/loving intentions to keep your home or yourself (body, mind, emotions and your auric field) cleansed so that you and your surroundings remain on higher vibrations.

*Note- you can clear space and your body with actual sage, rose oil or rose water. A mixture of herbs or essences is a great way to cleanse too. These can be applied to the body, inhaled or spritzed! These are just add-ons. You have to use intention of thought when using them. "They are clearing me- my body, my aura and my space."

We are all made up of energy, everything is made of energy. Energy is vibrations. Vibrations of high frequency are not necessarily louder, but are cleaner. An example is when you are happy, your vibrational energy or frequency is higher. When you are not in a great mood, your vibrations or energy field is of lower frequency. The lower frequency can be emotions such as feeling stuck, worried, frightened, sad or depressed.

Where I'm going with this is that when your own body is physically, mentally, emotionally, or spiritually on a higher vibration, you are "clearer." You probably think better, look better and feel better. Right? Right. I'm sure you've been there, but may not have understood. The same thing goes with space, like your home, for example. If everyone is grumpy in your home the energy vibration is lower, so it "feels" yucky. So by clearing that space not only can you clear that energy from the room, but you can also add energy that is of higher vibration. Intention also is used with clearing.

Remember even a thought that was not spoken aloud is an energy vibration, so make that thought of happy, higher vibrations. I always channel to clients that *"You rule your mind,"* the guides say, *"You decide if you are happy or sad. You choose to make today high vibration; it is always you who makes the choice, no one else."*

You can cleanse or clear several ways. You can cleanse by sage-ing the room, saying an affirmation, asking for guided assistance from spirits or angels to help clear. You can also use your good, loving intentions to visualize the room as clean and clear with high vibration energy. A fun way to clear is to use sound by using a singing bowl, didgeridoo, or tuning forks. Reiki is also useful to clear yourself and your home or just thinking happier thoughts, releasing any stresses you have. Stress is negative energy, which is lower vibration, so removing the stress can help clear. Finally, you can do a relaxing meditation to clear yourself and keep you personally on higher vibration. The key is to get to a higher vibration and stay there—don't bring negative in! You don't need to do all of these things, just choose whatever method of clearing you like best and works with your lifestyle, but remember that loving intention with all of these ways is the proper way to "clear space." I show you more details on the next pages on clearing exercises and how to release.

I also would like to emphasize that you are a clearer channel or conduit without the use of drugs or alcohol. It is common sense never to communicate when intoxicated. This can lower your vibration and distort your energy. If you are a person that works with energetic healing, please respect others by being a clean and clear channel with your work. Remember: Good Intention, Intention, and Intention!

7 Protection

Protecting yourself is important to ensure that you can be safe while exploring your intuitiveness because there are lower vibration people and entities that may cross your path.

As you may believe or not, there are entities out there, not just Earthly ones, that are not nice. Just like that real human person that hustled you out of your hard earned money or cut in front of you or screamed at you for no reason. There are some of those energies in different dimensional planes too. So this is where you ask your Angels, the universe or your source, and protect with good intentions.

You can protect yourself in several ways. Using your Intention and reciting an affirmation is a good way. I like to ask to be "clear, cleansed, balanced, and protected in the name of the Light." That is one of my favs.

You should protect yourself from negative energies such as thought forms, which are negative thoughts that others project on you out of jealousy, anger or their own problems they wish on someone else, and that someone could be you (these are called self-sabotage thoughts).

If you encounter any of these negative vibrations, you will "feel" it. You can feel the energy to be uncomfortable, heavy, creepy, or just a plain bad feeling! As soon as this happens, whether the source is coming from this Earth, meaning a human, or an entity from somewhere else, protect by saying a prayer or affirmation of positive vibrations. You can ask the universe or your source to help relieve you of this lower vibration. At the same time, you can also imagine white or gold light over your entire body and you can say the mantra I was given by EROM, St. Germaine and the Light Ones, *"oh Lahhh me oh Lahhh protection of life, petals of life."* Say this mantra 3 times and you will feel the protection and safe feeling come over you. Some people describe it as a "whoosh" that cleansed them and the space they were currently at. I also wrote a prayer I use to keep myself protected when and if I need it. You are welcome to use this also:

Please, may I ask God, source, Universal Light (or whomever you believe in) to please come and keep me clean, clear and protected in the name of the light.

From this moment forward, you can say the time and location. **For example**, *"8:11 am, Boca Raton, Florida, Earth in all dimensions, all levels, to be of light, and surrounded by light, until all of eternity. Anything other than the light will leave immediately from [your name] physically, mentally, emotionally and spiritually on all levels and all dimensions. Thank you for your protection. I am grateful."*

Make sure you are very specific with your protection to get your best results.

8 Renewable Energy

Yes, I know it sounds like a service company- but this Renewable energy is all about "calling back." This means to call back your energy that may have been depleted by other energies, such as other people with low vibrational energy. You can ask to call it back from your source (God, the Light, Universe, the moon etc.).

You can do this easily. If you are good at visualization you can imagine this energy from the light coming from your source, filling your body, starting at your crown above your head, into your head, inside and out, your face, neck, back, down your arms, each finger, chest, stomach, hips, thighs, knees, calves, and to every toe. Imagine this white or golden light covers you completely and fills you up inside and out. I personally like to picture this as water or liquid dripping over me, re-energizing my every cell. I then thank my source, the light, and immediately feel more energetic. I also say, *"I am clean, clear and balanced, physically emotionally, mentally and spiritually. I am grateful. Anything other than the light will go out of my body into the Earth to be recycled and renewed. My energy is replaced with love and light, keeping me happy, healthy and protected."*

That's it! I usually do this every morning as I'm showering. It's really easy to visualize this because I can see and feel the water over my body, then I imagine it inside cleaning and renewing energies within my body. I even do this easy and fast exercise when around a lot of energies (people mostly that are draining). What I do is excuse myself to the ladies room and begin recharging. I come back and feel much better! Try it! So, when those energy suckers come, you can take 5 minutes and recharge!

9 Beliefs

All that you do is important, and if you feel happier and more fulfilled, then that is a beautiful way of life.

Enjoy your time on this Earthly plane and make the best of every situation. Most of us tend to make mountains out of molehills, and I'm guilty of that but when I become mindful of that, I totally turn it around and see the good of what might have happened for me or for the good of another. Remember everything is not all about you. Leaving our egos behind is quite hard, but when you do, you will feel and see the difference it makes in your life. You can let go of things like jealousy. It truly is amazing. You become happier with "you." You feel more content with what you have and have to offer yourself physically and mentally. It's like this beautiful gift inside us, that we just need to release, or open that window so we can see it clearly. You need to show your higher vibrations and happiness to yourself and the world around you, and of course beyond. The more you open your mind and beliefs, the more you can explore and decide what is right for you.

You may not believe all you hear from gurus and psychics, but that may be because that information was meant for them and others, but not you. You are meant to experience, feel, or hear what is right for you and your life from "you." The expression "different strokes for different folks" applies here!

Basically, you must believe in yourself and be able to identify what is positive and trust yourself to believe in that. Believe in positive vibrations and positive information.

10 Explore

Continue to explore. Exploration is the key to finding what modalities are right for you. Maybe you want to learn Reiki for self-healing. Maybe you just want to know about it or possibly you want or feel the need to help others with it as a profession. You may also be feeling you need to know more so you can teach and spread what you have learned and add to what you had already felt.

Begin to open up to hear what others say or experience. Make life more fun and exciting. Allow yourself to open up to conversations with other people. You can find enjoyment with other people and then share your experiences. Your shared stories and experiences may help each other. Experiences make us well-rounded. Take a chance and live outside your box.
And before you do… know this

Chapter 4
What's an Aura? What are Chakras?
Cord-cutting, attachments and clearing your aura.

What's an Aura?
The aura is an electromagnetic field that surrounds the outer body. Our auras have many layers. Auras are also scientifically known.

An aura is described as **"an electromagnetic field (also EMF or EM field)**). This information is by Wikipedia. **Their version states: a physical** field **produced by** electrically charged objects. **It affects the behavior of charged objects in the vicinity of the field. The electromagnetic field extends indefinitely throughout space and describes the** electromagnetic interaction. **It is one of the four** fundamental forces **of nature (the others are** gravitation, **the** weak interaction, **and the** strong interaction**).**

The field can be viewed as the combination of an electric field **and a** magnetic field. **The electric field is produced by stationary charges, and the magnetic field by moving charges (currents); these two are often described as the sources of the field. The way in which charges and currents interact with the electromagnetic field is described by** Maxwell's equations **and the** Lorentz force law.

From a classical **perspective, the electromagnetic field can be regarded as a smooth, continuous field, propagated in a wavelike manner; whereas from the perspective of** quantum field theory, **the field is seen as quantized, being composed of individual** particles.**"**
My compliments to Wikipedia for this information above written in bold print.

Back to my version …
Our body's aura/energy field is something everyone should be schooled about. Knowing and understanding how it works is amazing, yet simple.

Think of your physical body- I want you to realize that we also have this additional part of our body. That is the aura. Most people cannot visually see the human aura. The aura *is* part of our body. Unfortunately, in grade school, anatomy classes didn't teach us about our energetic bodies.

I hope in the near future the school systems recognize the importance of the human energetic body as one with our physical bodies of flesh and bones.

It seems many doctors are finally finding this to be relevant in relating physical illnesses with vibrational energetics. The correlation between the two are becoming more main-stream in healing modalities. Kudos to those docs!

Auras work with our energy centers. They are called "Chakras"

Our auras work with our energy centers. These energy centers are vortexes within our bodies and in our energetic field. I know it sounds confusing. These chakras/energy centers and our aura can balance our emotions and our physical body on many levels. The vortexes are spinning and create balance. They are basically vibrations of healthy or unhealthy frequencies.

A bit more on
Chakras &
our Energy Exchange with our human bodies

The 7 main energy centers called chakra points
are as shown in this picture supplied by clip art.

CHAKRAS
Chakras are energy centers that are located down the center of a person's body along the meridian or spinal column. These wheel or disc-like centers are also associated with colors for each chakra point. There are 7 main chakras but there are over 144,000 chakras in the human body. . These are energy centers that constantly open and close on a day to day basis.

Each chakra represents a center point in the human body which can energize, release, hold or vibrate. These energy centers constantly open and close during the day. This is normal, but keeping them balanced is the key to being a balanced human. When I say balanced, I mean physically, mentally, emotionally and spiritually balanced.

When humans are unbalanced in any one of these areas they can be over compensating in another area of the body. If a chakra is out of place- for a long period of time, sickness can manifest. This could be as physical, mental, emotional or spiritual. So keeping *yourself* and your energy centers /chakras aligned and balanced is a must.

The chakra at the base of the spine is called the **root or 1st chakra**. This chakra represents 'grounding". The **2nd chakra is named the sacral** -representing "survival, instinct", the **3rd chakra is solar plexus** representing "personal power or EGO.

The **4th chakra -the heart**, representing love and compassion. The **5th chakra is the throat** chakra representing communication, expression, and creativeness and also listening.

 The 6th chakra representing the "third eye" or mind's eye. This represents intuitiveness and trusting in yourself.

Lastly is the **7th chakra**- which represents connection to your higher self and other beings of light. This higher –self is the all knowing you-you can connect with the celestial plane of Angels, Spirit guides, and humans that have passed over or on other dimensions.

The more you know about your body the more it can help you stay balanced. It is a good energy exchange that balances you on the physical, emotional and mental levels.

Taking good care of your physical body is part of the exchange as well. You most likely feel healthier or "better" when you eat foods that are known as natural or organic, basically unprocessed. That is a positive energy exchange with your insides and outside on the physical level. Your chakras are the example of the perfect energy exchange on an energetic level.

Sync-up

The human aura works in synchronicity with our energy centers. Chakras and auras work together for balancing our bodies.

You will find an energy session is a healthy, alternative method for cleansing the energy in one's body. Think of it as a monthly maintenance.

One method is using a form of *energy healing* to keep our bodies' aura clean and clear. This clarity keeps us aligned and balanced to feel great.

There are many types of energy healing modalities that cleanse our bodies. Here are a few examples: Reiki healing and Light Tunnel Energy ™ channeled mandalas, crystal healing and guided meditations. When these modalities are performed properly they can positively re- align and balance your chakras and clean your auric field. For more information on these modalities go to my website Jolie DeMarco.com

Are there other kinds of attachments?

Sure. You mean other than thoughts and emotions from people or animals?

Yes, but they do involve emotions:

There can be attachments to tangible things. Here is

 my **best example-** a house.

Let's say you are trying to sell your home. It looks great, priced correctly, but nothing is working on getting this home sold. I've got one word for you-

purpose. The house has purpose. You may want it sold, but what about the other family members? Maybe your kids don't want to move and they are placing mega emotions within the home's aura. You can help the kids feel good about moving, by explaining it's a new adventure, this may help them release the house. Then the home can *feel good* to potential buyers and you can get it sold.

If it is just you living there, you may have an unconscious emotion that is attached to it. Maybe you had a relationship in that home that you aren't yet giving up on- this I call a "double attachment." The home and you are holding relationship energy.

Here's another example. A client wanted to be rehired at her previous job as a teacher; she was not hired back and without any known reasons- to her knowledge. She was however looking for another job and could not land one. She was well qualified for many positions she applied for. She realized that she had an attachment to the last job, **since she *did not have closure* on why** she was not rehired the next year. She then did a soul talk with the principal. She felt relief and got the closure she needed to move forward. She is now working at a great school.

Another example:
Having an attachment to your work! You know that relationship of you and your workplace. Working over and beyond, eating and talking about work all the time, dreaming about work during your sleep! This is a sign of an unhealthy attachment. You need a life, a balanced life!
 Here's a surefire way to know if you have an unhealthy attachment to work.
Ask yourself these questions:

- Do I work more than 10 hours a day?
 -Do I think about work when I am eating?
 -Do I talk to my friends or partners and mention work more than once in a visit or conversation?

 If this is you- release this unhealthy relationship with work. I'm not asking you to quit your job, just to be unattached when you get home and sleep! Get a hobby; take a class that takes the thought of work out of your mind. You can release the overworking patterns by self-soul talking.

About cleansing yourself from thought forms and attachments

What is cleansing and clearing?

Some people need to *release* unwanted energies from their bodies. When someone needs to let -go or clear themselves- it means they need to cleanse their electro-magnetic field (aura) around their body. It can also mean they need to cleanse their chakras.

If you are unsure of how you feel –or may feel as if you are carrying emotional weight on your hips or shoulders -this can also indicate a person's body needs an energetic or physical healing. An emotional or mental healing can also be felt in the aura by trained professionals.

Can I clear myself?
Yes. Keep reading. I explain how.

What gets in our aura that makes it negative or heavy?

When debris is in our energy field, "in your space" or aura, that usually means negative emotions or "junk" may be deep within the auric fields. Sometimes this junk can be multi-dimensional. This is when a person may need a "cord cutting with replacement, or a deeper release. "

This is energy terminology. An energy healing is administered energetically by removing negative vibes and replacing with positive vibes.

This is for a person who needs to relieve themselves from negative vibrations or junk in their auric field. A person that feels depressed, upset, anxious, angry, fearful, sick or unbalanced would benefit from an energy healing session.

One example is a *cord cutting*. This type of energy healing session allows the negative energy to be released instead of imprinting in the soul. After which, the practitioner should replace the negative energy that was "cut out" with positive energy.

This way the energy that was unwanted is gone and that **voided space** immediately filled with positive energy.

You can also do a cord cutting and replacement on your own. The spirit guides call this technique **"soul talking"**. This self-healing is the best way to advance in your life and feel great.

The purpose of this cleansing and clearing is to feel free of *old or stuck energies that can be mental, emotional, physical or spiritual.*

Cleansing and clearing releases "you" of that heavy emotional weight or negative thoughts, worries, and patterns that are unhealthy!

Some of these thoughts and emotions could be placed on you by other people- consciously or sub-consciously. You can also absorb or pick-up negative emotions from other people walking past you. You can also pick up someone else's junk by stepping into another person auric field.

Why are there other people's emotions in <u>my</u> aura?

You could be an empath. This is a person who can physically feel emotions and/or ailments of others in their own physical body and/or auric field.

On a daily basis we pick up other peoples "stuff." You can be an empath, sensitive person or an average Joe-we all pick up junk. This includes other people's emotions. Some of us can pick up other peoples physical "hurts"-as well as emotional feelings.

For example: if your girlfriend calls you and tells about her negative feelings of her day- she dumped her negative emotions on you.

You may feel bad for her; some people will actually want to take hurt away from their friend and subconsciously take over her problems. This is taking on other people's "stuff" and owning it.

Another example: a person who can be in large crowd of people and suddenly out of the blue, they will feel sick to their stomach. This "sick" feeling may be another person's emotional or physical pain.

Not everyone is empathic in a strong way-but we can all certainly use a clearing and cleansing of our auras.

Since most people cannot visually see debris within their aura- routine clearing is best. All of us pick up debris on a daily basis- it just happens as we interact with others in our regular lives.

Can someone put a spell on me? Or place bad Ju Ju/voodoo on me?

Really? You want to ask that? Okay listen. I want to explain it like this: If energy is only positive, negative or null- as we discussed earlier- then yes someone can place a negative thought form in your aura.

Yes they can.

BUT- in my experience and my opinion- If you know how powerful you are- you can rid the negative ju ju. You can "intentionally" accept or NOT accept negative energy.

You may receive an unwanted negative cloud in your aura from a person that has negative thoughts towards you- or basically hates your guts- you can dismiss it.

However, you can **choose** to notice this negative energy in your field and release it.

You can also choose to empower it. Only YOU can make it grow. Using your own negative emotion called "fear".

My suggestion is to **think** like I do. I recognize the negative "yucks" and release them. Then I immediately imagine Angels replacing the voided space with beautiful songs.

 In my mind- I see positive energy as a visual image of Angels.

My visual image of negative is a minus sign. Just like in math. This is a minus sign- can you see that? Good. When you feel negative, know it consists of a minus sign.

 I <u>don't allow</u> my mind to make the negative feeling into a scary monster or voodoo. Refrain from allowing the emotion of fear or anything scary to come to you and build. Ya know, don't make a mountain (devil) out of a mole hill (a minus sign).

Here is a technique you can do. You can say this in your mind or verbally out loud.
This is what I say:
"Anything other than the light- goes out of my physical body and out of my aura into the Earth to be recycled and renewed." Then I visualize a mini minus-sign for me to get rid of it.

I replace it as quick as I can with angels or anything positive. I *don't allow* the negatives to grow in my mind or auric field.

That is the Jolie "keep-away." Try it. This makes life waaaay easier.

As you practice this technique, you will find you will master it quicker and quicker. Eventually, all of your thoughts will go to the automatic pilot of positive only.

Remember there will always be people that are unhappy in life. Hopefully, sooner than later- they will change to positive ways. Some people like to emit and send negative junk to others.

They use bad intentions and spread it around thinking it is power. They are bad energy exchangers! Just know you can release all negatives- out of your body and energy field.

 You have the positive power of intention. That is what you desire and project. Enough said.

Can I clear myself? Can I clean my aura?

Yep. This is simple- if you can feel or visualize. If you cannot visualize, it's okay. Everyone can feel- sense or imagine. This **intent** enables everyone to clear their own body, mind and auric field. **Intention**

Power!

To clear your auras on a daily basis follow these instructions.

Step 1. Imagine/visualize or feel the heaviness- all the negative feelings and "junk". Notice where. Sense the specific places in your body that you sense the negative feelings or emotions. This I call "identifying."

Step 2 .Then imagine/visualize or feel- all the negative junk that is currently present in your energy field (aura). Now —move it all out of your body and your aura. Imagine pushing all the junk out of your space. Feel all of that debris going out of you and into the ground. Imagine all of that going into mother Earth to be recycled and renewed for you.

I visualize the junk and debris to be grey mini clouds in my aura; I flush them down past my feet, then into Earth. Sometimes I grab them and toss' em down into the ground.

Step 3. Then imagine or feel your body and aura being squeaky clean. Clean and clear.

 Shower time!

Is it hard for you to visualize?

This example is better for those people that have a hard time with visualizing. When a person feels the water over their body- it becomes a 'feeling" you can relate to cleansing.

Another option to cleanse yourself:

You can rid yourself of negative clouds in your aura. Do this is while you are in the shower. Most of us take showers daily. When you clean your body- You also can clean your auric field. Allowing the yuck and dirty grey clouds to go down the drain with the water.

Step 4. Now imagine/visualize replacing that space that was holding the "yuck stuff" with beautiful thoughts or words or visions. That "yucky junk" went out of your aura. Now replace it by saying positive words, thoughts or visions.

I am happy
I am balanced
I love myself
I am love and I am surrounded by love

A great vision-go to a happy place. Visualize a gorgeous happy place. I use Hawaii as my happy place. I see myself looking over the ocean from a beautiful mountain, lush waterfalls and serenity. Choose your place.

Remember, if you use a *happy place* visualization- it is a happy place –that means **_no people in it_** but YOU! Otherwise, the other people can bring **emotions** that aren't so happy in your joyous place.

More than meets the eye

Check out the drawing of the human aura. You can visualize what affects us. This picture shows what most human eyes cannot see.

This will help you understand what you may feel and sense.

Yes! The stick figure is supposed to represent a human person! The circle around the human is their aura! I know you are laughing at my picture...
Remember attachments are just emotions that are vibrations fromyourself and from other energies- that can be people, places anything that is energy.

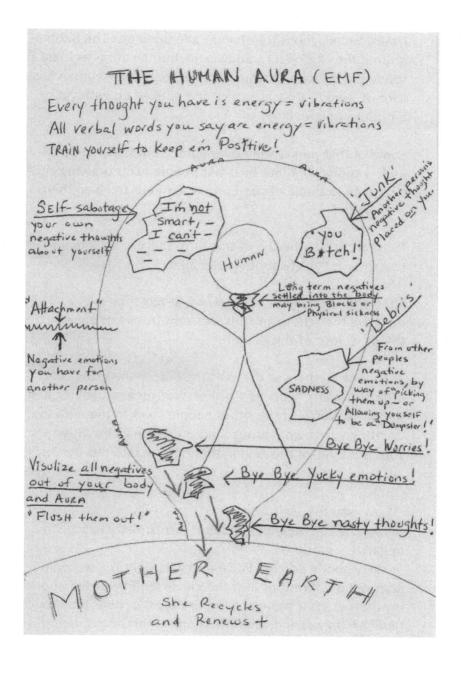

THE HUMAN AURA (EMF)

Every thought you have is energy = vibrations
All verbal words you say are energy = vibrations
TRAIN yourself to keep 'em Positive!

AURA   AURA

'Junk' Another persons negative thought placed on you.

SELF-sabotage
your own
negative thoughts
about yourself

I'm not
smart, —
I can't —
— — —

you
B*tch!

Human

Long term negatives settled into the body may bring Blocks or Physical sickness

'Debris'

"Attachment"

Negative emotions
you have for
another person

SADNESS

From other peoples negative emotions, by way of "picking them up — or Allowing yourself to be a Dumpster!"

Bye Bye Worries!

Visulize all negatives
out of your body
and AURA
"FlusH them out!"

Bye Bye Yucky emotions!

Bye Bye nasty thoughts!

MOTHER EARTH

She Recycles
and Renews +

I want to talk about this handmade drawing . The bubble around the stick figure body is the human aura- as I said. Inside the bubble- is a human. This particular human has a lot of "junk!" They are stuck and gunked up with yucky emotions and feelings.

Some of that junk is their own doing -and some of that junk was placed there by other people. This drawing shows an example of someone who needs to clean their aura badly!

First . Notice at the top of the aura- there is an "I'm not smart- I cant" self-sabotage thought.

Then you see a cloud of the word "b-tch" that was a negative thought form. This was sent from someone else that is jealous of this person.

Then look all the way down at the bottom near the feet area.These are "worries. " These worries are also negative thoughts.Worries from other people stuck in the aura too. Creating your own worries holds negative vibes within your aura. All of this is junk that is stuck into this person's aura.

 Wow- see the "self worry."
 All worries are negative thought forms. Yes. That means negative vibrations.
 A story about worries. Since every thought is a worry,it goes out as vibrations into the universe. If I worried about my mother, that thought form or negative vibes would find her. If I worried with intentionally thinking of her or whomever the intent can direct those vibes to reach that person. I used to do that a lot. Worry about stuff in

general. Once I realized that was basically sending negative vibes all over town, I stopped myself.

There was one person I worried about all the time (and will remain nameless lol). When I learned how energy works and decided to change the worried thoughts to positive thoughts such as :" they are perfectly fine - happy, healthy and safe." Guess what? That nameless person actually looked healthier and became healthier since I sent positive to them instead of negative to them. I know sometimes subconsciously we worry, but that's why *we all need to be mindful not mindless.*
Now I am only sending positive, healthy vibes to people I think about.

How do I get rid of worries?

Easy. Re-train the brain to think differently. I like to imagine there is a worry channel- just like a TV or radio. This *worry* channel *is negative.* Negative is no good to anyone. I decided to change this "negative channel" to a better, happpier one. *I choose* to use my happy positive channel.

Just change your radio station!

When I start to think of a worry — it can be about me or a worry about someone else- I quickly turn the channel from the "negative worry channel" to the "happy positive channel."

I imagine tuning into a better radio station! I confirm this new positive channel by saying " I am perfectly fine and well" or "I am happy and healthy."

Let's say you are starting to put that "worry channel back on –" maybe it's a worry of your mother or sister- just – Stop. Change those thoughts or words. Tune- in into the positive station!

 Then send those people -your mom, father, sister,son, daughter, whomever- a positive thought form. Here's a positive thought form to send out. Think or verbally say:" my mom,dad and sister are happy and healthy." Voila- it is that easy.

It works because if you are diligent with this "changing the channel" You made that thought into an action." You can master the training. You actually get tired of changing the channel back and forth. Finally, you decide to keep it on the happy positive one permanently.

Back to the drawing…

In the aura drawing- do you see the "attachment" ?

 We can have positive or negative attachments. As written on previous pages-there is one particular thing I would like to point out. If you are holding a negative attachment **_and_** you are currently single and looking- this next bit of information is for you!

If you want to meet a **"good match"**- your chances are slim to null - *if* you have a negative attachment.

Simply because a ***good match*** respects you and you them. This is an equal or positive energy exchange. Anyone that truly respects ***you***- would not ask ***you*** out on a date- if you were "taken and /or attached."

Remember me talking about how people can feel and sense things from each other? Without trying to read energy? Okay good. Because this example *is* what I am explaining to you. To other people you may appear and feel-like your energy is "taken."

Example: You may currently have an old emotional attachment to an old boyfriend or girlfriend or ex- As this new person that is your *good match*- walks by you and unknowingly senses you.. they can sense "taken."Since they are *within* your energy bubble(aura.)

This potential *good match* can sense and may *think* to themselves:"Oh he/she is HOT-but they must be married or have a girlfriend/boyfriend."

They are sensing you are 'taken". They are feeling this because you are " energetically taken"-with that emotional string attached to your side!

How can I say this plainly ...YOU ARE MISSING YOUR OPPERTUNITY TO MEET YOUR GOOD MATCH- IF YOU HAVE A NEGATIVE ATTACHEMENT!

You will attract _those relationships that you don't want_ -if you keep the attachement- while you are "looking".

That was loud. Hopefully clear.

Okay a refresher:

1. Keep your energy clear.

2. At anytime you feel yucky or cannot identify how you feel- Clear your aura- flush the junk out of you!

3. Stop the self –sabotage thoughts and replace them with positive actions, thoughts or visions.

4. Let go of the worries- say a positive mantra-" I am happy and healthy."

5. If you feel sick physically or intuitively- imagine moving the pain or *difference*
out of your body- out of your energy field-Yes -flush it again!

Let's Talk Relationships

Chapter 5

Let's talk relationships.
Interesting stuff that *matters*
Fear be gone- the No Regret Rule
Angel Messages

Relationships can be:

-Current that needs mending
-Great relationships
-Nonexistence relationships
-Relationships that are attachments
-Faux relationships
-Relationships that need closure
-Okay, but not fulfilling relationships
-Relationships without passion

Everything goes back to the energy exchanges in your life.
Relationships are energy exchanges.

First we are going to explore your personal relationship with a significant other. If this doesn't apply to you, I ask you to continue to read it anyway! This may give you some insight to help a friend.

Oh, those relationships that need closure or newness.
How to be sure this relationship is the right choice?

Well, when this happens there are a few things you can do.
First answer these questions to know if this is truly where you are at with this relationship.
Ask yourself:

1. Do you feel like you didn't get an explanation why there was a break-up?
2. Did they just leave? Did you just leave?
3. Are you together, yet never *or* barely talk?
4. Were they or are they disloyal in what was once a monogamous relationship?
5. Were you disloyal to them?
6. Are you unhappy and think about leaving the relationship?
7. Did your chemistry just fizzle or you/they feel unattractive?
8. Are there constant misunderstandings?

Now that you know a little bit more about yourself, we can go on to this next exercise.

If you answered yes to any of the above- you need to get a pen and paper.

 1. Write down how you really feel. Yes, write it you can toss it after. You need to get this junk out of your energy field and out of your body. You can curse and cry. Do it.

2. Next I want you to make a deal with yourself to try the *"pre-no regret rule."* You have to agree to do it with positive intention.

I call it the "pre-regret rule" because it is a prerequisite before you go for the no regret rule; it proves you are serious about this! Remember no bull! This is your life and your relationship; it affects you and another person!

This is called the "Pre-no regret <u>rule</u>. "

For the next month, you will write one word when you wake up and one before you go to bed. The one word is how you feel.

Example I wake up in the am, I feel good. I feel refreshed. Maybe you feel exhausted.

Just write it.

When you are ready to go to sleep, you write one word or a few.

Here is an example: I feel freakin' pissed, I'm aggravated. Maybe you feel incredible or this is the best day ever.

Okay you got this. It will help you to get insight on yourself and who or what makes you feel "off."

This is a super easy task and will save you tons at a psychiatrist.

 After one month, you will look back and see if you have any patterns in the days you felt positive vs negative.

Remember maybe you were or were not around a certain person, or thinking of that person.

Hint, hint.

If you already know that things are not right or *absolutely* positive between you and this other person, you can *skip* the pre regret and start here.

You will go directly to the **no regret <u>test.</u>**
You are totally ready for this- big time.
Let's say you love this person, but aren't in love with them at least that's what you think right now or this week.

 ### *Looking through each other eyes*
Go ahead, put yourself in their shoes.
Would you want someone to be with *you*

that doesn't love you 100%?
 Would you want to be #2?
Most of you will say" heck no, I'm *not* number 2. I'm number one or not at all."
 Okay, let us proceed. No matter if you love them or hate them at this point, *you or they* do not want or deserve to be number 2.

Looking through their eyes and looking through yours makes it easy to understand.
 No-one wants to be #2.
This is a clear sign that there is a respect issue between both of you.
The **no regret test** allows you to *truly know* that you are making the correct decision whether it be staying and mending the relationship or going your separate ways.

The NO Regret test

Step 1. Please do the *soul talking* with this person. (Refer to chapter 7) Take your time, this is important. After which, take a few days or so to evaluate how you feel once more. It is common to feel emotional changes after a soul talk session. This can bring you great clarity.
Step 2. After two to three days. Evaluate again. Notice what and how you feel about yourself and the other person.

Step 3. You now have 2 options to decide upon: option A or B to proceed. Please read both options as this will help you take the correct path for you at this time in your life about this particular relationship. Here is one to live by- *Respect and honor thyself and others.*

Option A.

If you feel you are still unsure of what you want out of the relationship, it's time to make the **no regret test** your option. Option A is allowing the forward motion.

You do this by agreeing with yourself, that you will give this person 2-3 months of you giving 100% of your efforts into this relationship. Please do not share this *test* with the person you are deciding about, this can cause them to only be good for that time frame- which would be a false positive!

You will see over this time period if you get an equal energy exchange. This is sometimes hard because you have to be the one to give it your all first. Release the ego and step-up my friends.

The results

After the 1-3 months, whatever you are comfortable with as far as time, you will truly see if you got the 100% back from that relationship partner.

It is super important that you truly want to make the 100% effort with good true intentions. Being fake isn't helping anyone.

If you *did not* receive your 100% efforts back, then you have your test completed. You will never have to think that you should've, would've, could've. Because *you did*, you gave it 100% and you did not get it back. You know that the respect and value is not there for you with this relationship. The relationship is not mutual. Clarity at last.

If you received your 100% back or close enough to it *and* you feel happy- yeahhh!! All it took was a bit of you showing more value, love, respect and compassion to be mutually recognized.

Option B

Option B. If you are 100 % sure you want to re-work the relationship then verbally talk to the person and let them know how you are feeling and use key words like "we", don't single them out with blame. Ask if they are ready to re-new and make a better life together by starting over and forgetting about all the past junk and making a pact that both of you will not bring up past issues. Starting new, new goals together, new ways of communication and setting the sparks in all ways by doing new fun things of interest together. This is something you both have to agree. Don't imagine they are agreeing if they do not. This is important. This has to be mutual.

The energy exchanges between you equal, both hearing each other and listening to each other. Respect and value each other to a "normal" you both accept as positive.

Here's a fun **30 second** renew it *thang*

 You are going to need two note pads and two pens, and your cell phone to use as a timer or an old style click clock timer. Hand your partner a pad and pen, set the timer for 30 seconds. Now ask your partner to write as many things as they can of dreams or something they would love to do *without overthinking*. Stress the words," as many as you can" in 30 seconds.

I express this because if it's longer than 30 seconds, usually people tend to over think and over rationalize and the dreams aren't really dreams they are too thought out.

Back to the buzzer. The 30 seconds are up; you both will switch notepads and read what each other wrote on them. Yep, you guessed it, there will be stuff on there you never knew the other wanted to do. Now you have something *new* to talk about. How 'bout that. *Refreshing,* isn't it? Just letting go of the monotony of your lives to *dream*-this is an exercise that allows it. If it's possible, why not try to make one of their dreams come true. Then pick one of

yours as well. This is a great energy exchange and appositive a *goal* to do *together*.
Dreams are fuel for vitality and life.

I'm just making a point

Some of you may be thinking that you don't feel sexually connected to your significant other, due to lack of all the stuff we talked about previously. I would like to shine this idea your thoughts and perception. This is only *if* you are one that is taking action to mend your relationship.

Here it is: You most likely know someone that has first dated a person and they had no physical attraction to them. Then after dating a few weeks, they *became* attracted to that person. This was because they got to know the person. Can you relate?

Okay, here is another example: Have *you* or have you known someone that fell in love with a best friend or co-worker? It was *not* love at first sight, but the passion grew because of commonalities. Hmmm...have you known or heard of this happening? Just say, yes!

My point is- if you are in a current relationship that needs mending, and *you* continuously say or think that you are *not* attracted to that person; you are programming that negative affirmation. If you *try* and *re-think, re-program* and mend the relationship, you can fall in love with them again. Since you did fall in love once before. Or you can pretend like you just met and start everything new from scratch. That can be fun☺. I call this a new beginning!

Do you get the correlation of my examples and my point?

Get to know each other again.

A little somethin'

Did we talk about tones?

I know this may come to you as a surprise, but many of us talk with underlying tones that may not be as desirable as we think. How so?

Are you not being heard by others?

I would bet ya *that you think* they are just not listening to you because of what you are saying. I beg to differ. I would bet it's really because the *tone* you are using. Here is an example.

When I was a little girl, I was upstairs in my room playing a lot. My mom would call my name to come downstairs. If she called me in a sweet voice by saying "Jolie, get down here." I would run down thinking she made me cookies! If my mom used a tone that was a harsher vibe, and said the same words- I knew oh crap, I'm in trouble-

However, words do matter, if you know the true definition of them *and* the people around you know the same definition as you.

Words-The Earth is a melting pot of ethnicities

Hope is that we all have common definitions of our words. Words of love, gratitude, intention, honor and respect. If all of us can realize and have an understanding that these powerful words in all languages, decency would rise and harmony would be common. Know these words for their true value and meaning and the vibrations they emit.

Gratitude is loving intent from one soul to another soul.

Intention is what you desire and project.

Honor is being worthy and loved.

Respect is actions, words or thoughts that are positive to you and other people.

Tools

I hope you utilize the tools I shared with you. Guidance from those above and from my experiences of relationships is about learning and sharing. We learn through experiences. They are sometimes good sometimes bad. If we remember the lessons and don't repeat the bad stuff, we move forward. This helps us to share with other people and help their lives be easier too.

My guides always say that *humans make life so complicated*. They say we as humans have wonderful relationships. Some last a lifetime. Some are meant to be transitional. They say we should listen to our bodies and minds and we will be shown the best way. Unfortunately, we humans have selective hearing.

> "I *choose* & allow myself to live happily.
> I am the keeper of my soul."

Angel Messages about The Energy Exchange

Please read the messages on the next pages to learn about the energy exchanges in Earthly life. Earlier in the book I explained I clairaudiently hear messages from Angels. These are quoted messages that are unedited and written exactly as they were received. Many of the messages are self-explanatory. I added my take on them.

I would also like *you* to interpret them - in your words. This helps you learn how you perceive things. Remember there is no right or wrong.

We all have different ways of reading and understanding. I believe that's what makes each one of us unique.

"Everything you do will have meaning-purpose."
"Adherently there are many obstacles in life- one is just a stone in a pond- that enjoys the company"

A human is surrounded by many trials in a huge world, but one person's love can make a big positive difference and be heard.

 "Energy surrounds everything in a human's life-make it positive"

Everything that exists is energy. All of us are made up of vibrations. Keep- em high vibes.

"Energy is simply positive and negative-choose positive

 High vibrations = happiness

"Choose the path that says, I am me."

We always have choices in life. Make decisions with "your" energy. Don't be something you really are not or not comfortable with.

"When lessons occur, it is more than one that learns. It is an equal energy exchange on levels. That sometimes one cannot necessarily "see' at that present moment"

We can be blinded with our emotions and not see the real truth. This is especially true because emotions are not plainly visible. We sometimes disregard listening to our emotional energy. We usually wait until we see physical proof. I also like to compare our understanding to a dirty window. Once we understand the concept of something- the window is *very clear* and clean. The window is now easy to see through.

"Speak to others kindly. As you receive what you place outwardly."
"Every thought is energy- notice how and what you think- that "thought energy" affects you and others that 'thought energy' is placed upon."

Thoughts are vibrations just like our physical voices.

I believe this refers to" thought forms." We can send or "place" energy of our thoughts on other people.

This is done simply by thinking something positive or negative and "sending" it their way/into their aura a.k.a. electromagnetic field around the human body.

The receiver- the person- can absorb this energy of that particular thought in their aura. This can affect them on an energetic level.

"It"- is not always about "you." There are many ways to "see" situations or feel emotions. Look through others eyes as well as your own."

Well, this is a great quote for all of *us* humans!

'Wise humans think positively in all situations.'
"Mindfulness is healthiness."

I always say and post on Facebook that there are *Mind-full* people and there are those people that choose *Mind-Less* acts.

"Understand only you, make decisions for you. You are the one that makes "choices." If you need to make an excuse- you will see your life decisions will reflect."

Amen to that.

"Sometimes a decision, a path can be hard. Knowing you always have a choice is freedom. A human is born with. Having a "mind" or thought of your own – is your personal power."

True. Although, we must learn to "use" our power in a good way and good timing is something to factor in.

"Share your compassion of being a "giver." Show or explain or guide to give others assistance, direction with empowerment.
"Doing everything for them diminishes their empowerment and is an un-balanced energy exchange for both of you."

"Accept help, support, advice or a compliment. Accepting is balanced energy exchange. Accepting is not taking- Realize this and your life will change for the best. The "Intention "of accepting is balanced- positive."

Accepting is not taking. Many of us do have to re-learn this one. This is a shout to all the over-givers out there- know your boundaries!

"The Intention of "taking" is unbalanced negative."

I asked these spirit guides, Can I make this a bumper sticker?

"Speak Kindly of others and think beautifully of yourself." Love thyself.

"Learn to have happy thoughts, experiences; positive energy makes you attractive on all levels."

Extremely true, who wants to be around a complainer or bummer attitude? Not I.

"Begin a new day with trying something different- it can be a new way to open your car door, a new kind of tea or coffee, or say hello to 5 people before you go to lunch- change monotony."

Meaning of Life
L- Learn
I-Identify
F-Find
E- Experience

Live outside your genie bottle. Enjoy life; it's full of fun surprises.

"Be – 'Aware' that Life is well and all around you –see the light and well-ness."

I interpret this as: Learn as much as you can. Experiences lead us to self-discovery, empowering oneself. Identify life around you with as much clarity as you can. Find new ways to savor and appreciate your life.

Interesting stuff

from Wikipedia

Matter is anything that occupies space and has rest mass (or invariant mass). It is a general term for the substance of which all physical objects consist.[1][2] Typically, matter includes atoms and other particles which have mass. Mass is said by some to be the amount of matter in an object and volume is the amount of space occupied by an object

In physics, **energy** (Ancient Greek: ἐνέργεια *energeia* "activity, operation"[1]) is an indirectly observed quantity that is often understood as the ability of a physical system to do work on other physical systems.[2][3] Since work is defined as a force acting through a distance (a length of space), energy is always equivalent to the ability to exert pulls or pushes against the basic forces of nature, along a path of a certain length.

The total energy contained in an object is identified with its mass, and energy cannot be created or destroyed. When matter (ordinary material particles) is changed into energy (such as energy of motion, or into radiation), the **mass** of the system does not change through the transformation process. However, there may be mechanistic limits as to how much of the matter in an object may be changed into other types of energy and thus into work, on other systems. Energy, like mass, is a scalar physical quantity. In the International System of Units (SI), energy is measured in joules, but in many fields other units, such as kilowatt-hours and kilocalories, are customary. All of these units translate to units of work, which is always defined in terms of forces and the distances that the forces act through.

A system can transfer energy to another system by simply transferring matter to it (since matter is equivalent to energy, in accordance with its mass). However, when energy is transferred by means other than matter-transfer, the transfer produces changes in the second system, as a result of work done on it. This work manifests itself as the effect of force(s) applied through distances within the target system. For example, a system can emit energy to another by transferring (radiating) <u>electromagnetic energy</u>, but this creates forces upon the particles that absorb the radiation. Similarly, a system may transfer energy to another by physically impacting it, but in that case the energy of motion in an object, called <u>kinetic energy</u>, results in forces acting over distances (new energy) to appear in another object that is struck. Transfer of <u>thermal energy</u> by <u>heat</u> occurs by both of these mechanisms: heat can be transferred by electromagnetic radiation, or by physical contact in which direct particle-particle impacts transfer kinetic energy.

Energy may be stored in systems without being present as matter, or as kinetic or electromagnetic energy. Stored energy is created whenever a particle has been moved through a field it interacts with (requiring a force to do so), but the energy to accomplish this is stored as a new position of the particles in the field—a configuration that must be "held" or fixed by a different type of force (otherwise, the new configuration would resolve itself by the field pushing or pulling the particle back toward its previous position).

This type of energy "stored" by force-fields and particles that have been forced into a new physical configuration in the field by doing work on them by another system is referred to as <u>potential energy</u>. A simple example of potential energy is the work needed to lift an object in a gravity field, up to a support. Each of the basic forces of nature is associated with a different type of potential energy, and all types of potential energy (like all other types of energy) appear as system <u>mass</u>, whenever present. For example, a compressed spring will be slightly more massive than before it was compressed. Likewise, whenever energy is transferred between systems by any mechanism, an associated mass is transferred with it.

Any form of energy may be <u>transformed</u> into another form. For example, all types of potential energy are converted into kinetic energy when the objects are given freedom to move to different position (as for example, when an object falls off a support).

When energy is in a form other than thermal energy, it may be transformed with good or even perfect efficiency, to any other type of energy, including <u>electricity</u> or production of new particles of matter. With thermal energy, however, there are often limits to the efficiency of the conversion to other forms of energy, as described by the <u>second law of thermodynamics</u>.

In all such <u>energy transformation</u> processes, the total energy remains the same, and a transfer of energy from one system to another, results in a loss to compensate for any gain. This principle, the <u>conservation of energy</u>, was first postulated in the early 19th century, and applies to any <u>isolated system</u>. According to <u>Noether's theorem</u>, the conservation of energy is a consequence of the fact that the laws of physics do not change over time.[4]

Although the total energy of a system does not change with time, its value may depend on the <u>frame of reference</u>. For example, a seated passenger in a moving airplane has zero kinetic energy relative to the airplane, but non-zero kinetic energy (and higher total energy) relative to the <u>Earth</u> .

I find these Wikipedia definitions to be comparative to some of what these Spirits of the light have shared about energy.

"I live in a world where everything has meaning" That is my quote on the subject.

Chapter 6

Inner Talk
Bad teacher *vs.* Superhuman

Inner talk can make or break ya

Okay I don't want to confuse you on this next one. Here's what is called self "inner talk". It's totally different than a soul talk. I just wanted to make that clear. Inner talk can be positive or negative. It rarely is null. Inner talk can make you or break you. It's that inner feeling or part of you that likes to give their 2 cents in most all of your situations in life. Especially, the emotional situations that you really would like some advice about.

I must confess I hear people using the term "selfie" and I was really thrown a bit since I *thought* that was something perverted. Until a young friend told me it is just taking a picture of yourself on a phone camera. Just in case you think like me, what I am writing about is called *self- inner talk, not a selfie*. Yeah I'm laughing☺

Super Human vs. Bad Teacher

You recently learned that everything is energy and everything has vibrations that can be positive, negative or null frequencies. Correct? Please say yes.
These vibes can affect your aura, other people and your emotions as well as your soul.

I can best explain your inner talking as   the **super human** part of you *and* the **bad teacher** part of you.

FYI

You don't want to be schooled by a bad teach. This teacher is negative and plays on your emotions in a not so cool way.
Bad teacher's inner talks are like this:
You suck, you aren't good enough, everyone is better looking than you, you are insecure, you are jealous, you can't do anything right and you get upset over everything!
Bad Teach plays on your fears and emotions that were learned behaviors that hold lower vibes.

Bad, bad, bad

This bad teacher likes to add tension to your life and brings confusion to your rational decisions. Bad teach especially loves to smack talk and tell you to do that with other people too. Bad teach wants to rule you by keeping you depressed and controlled. Here's one thing this teach loves to say" go ahead eat the whole cake; you don't need to share anything with anyone. Take, be afraid and always procrastinate with all that you do in life!"
 Bad teach makes your aura look like doo-doo. You are *not* the bright light everyone wants to hang out with but the one they stay away from.

Super-duper

On the fantastic other inner part of you is the *Super Human*; please imagine the high upbeat music in the background as you read this because that is how I am saying it. Super human is the bomb in a great way. Super human can squash bad teach in a second. Bad teach can start to talk and bam! Supahhh human kicked bad teach's ass out of town! All of those messages that were being programmed by bad teach are wiped out, 'cause super human came to save your butt- taking charge and puttin out those high vibes and happy thoughts, encouraging and empowering you to do good things and have great positive thoughts!

Powerful and strong -super human builds you up in a positive way, slammin' the door when bad teach comes a knockin.' Just think about it, if I walked up to you and said "hello my name is Jolie, and I am going to control you today," you would tell me off! No-one likes to be ruled or controlled. I'd rather go up to you and say "hello, my name is Jolie and I am going to show you how to empower yourself today."

UR Super Human Rocks!

We all want the perfect relationship, but ya gotta be ready to have one. Let's use the verbiage *good match relationship* instead of *perfect match.* Perfect match puts too much pressure on everyone. To have a good match relationship first you have to be the real you. Most people, after a breakup need to find their identity again, they need to find themselves.

What does that mean?

It's the about me thing. It is about you, so if you get yourself together to be balanced and strong as you once were you can be that balanced person you love, and so will everyone else. To be that person without anger or sadness, release the depressed thoughts and jealous junk. All of that stuff we talked about previously. You want the total you. Your energy, your aura, your body and mind to be clear and happy with high vibes-making you shine like that star or the bright moon in the sky. Yeah, that one- the *big* one. Cause when you shine your *good match* can find you and vice versa. Both of you can see the real you.

If you are ready, let's make ya shine. Do the soul talking with yourself and *you will feel it*.

Want to experience a self-soul clearing? Here's how.

Chapter 7

Soul Talking™ Techniques:
How to Soul Talk with you, how to Soul Talk with others- *ya feel it!*

The Earth's Moon Shift -A Meditation with You

This Earth moon shift meditation is a soul talk. It is an intense purposeful meditation for clearing your own soul's energy. You can release yourself from negative patterns, thoughts and energy that are no longer needed. Soul talking is an *awake style* of meditation.

How did this awake meditation emerge?
Since we are all made of energy - everything in the world is energy. Making equal energy exchanges is natural order. However, this order has been distorted with **entitlement issues among humans.** It's time to change that.

There was a shift that occurred in the year two thousand twelve and is continuing to year 2021. This second shift is about *how* people can re-learn to make positive, equal energy exchanges. This is why I call it the Earth's moon shift meditation.

The best way to express is with this quote: *"that all humans, everyone on Earth has reached a new vibration from the 2nd shift."* The Earth and moon shifted. It was due to cosmic events of a blue moon which actually means there were 2, separate, full moons in one month .This was and is rare. At that time of the 2nd shift those moons were profound in color. They had reddish outlines that you could see from looking up from Earth. Thereafter, there were 2 eclipses of the moon and star shower appeared.

During this beautiful event, I received messages from Spirit guides and Galileo: *"this is a shift of human energies with the energy exchange of the cosmos."*
Galileo said, since that moment- there are now *"new ways of asking"* for information- *"new ways to manifest."* He meant we (humans) could manifest what we would like or want to have in our lives. He also expressed to me clairaudiently that there are "**new ways of clearing.**"

This explains the true intention of performing a *soul talk*. Soul talking meditations are to release negative energy and then replace with positive energy. The purpose is to bring positive thoughts and feelings to make everything equal with all people and all existence.

Galileo and these other spirits shared that *"humans can heal themselves on many levels using energies of the cosmos and energies of light.* "I was *and I am* still impressed with these messages.

Below is one of the self- healing **soul talking** technique meditations they wanted us to utilize. It is a meditation that you are **fully awake and mindful.**

*Note- Please repeat the words- if you are comfortable with them. Make sure you are _using positive intention_ of what you feel, project and desire.

Use the intention that **you**- which is *your* true soul and *is* the pure energy and essence of "you."

It is important that you **accept and allow** the words you are thinking and verbally saying or visualizing and feeling in your body.

I suggest you print this out and read as you visualize. Another good idea: you can ask your friend to read this- so you can relax and really get into it. I suggest you go to a local wellness center and ask them to have a group session with this detailed information.

*Note- I have this meditation available on YouTube at Jolie DeMarco titled Soul Talking Technique if you would like to follow my voice for information about this meditation. If you need a little "push" to get going on your soul clearing process, you can find a Soul Talking Facilitator™ in your area to help you. http://www.SoulTalkingJolie.com. If you are ready now, follow the outline of this step by step instruction.

The Earth's moon shift meditation
SOUL TALKING WITH YOU

The term *"soul talking"* is a process that teaches people how to cleanse all their unwanted habits, thoughts, patterns and emotions from past, parallel and present. This will clear all the negatives from all that exists *within you*.

Step 1.
I am (say your full name.)
I allow my true soul, the energy of me-to engage with my human self, body and mind-
to soul talk with my true soul energy- *all that I am energy, on all dimensions , all parallels, all that My energy exists- all energies of me in all locations.*

Step 2. Take 11 deep breaths in and 11 long breaths out.

Step 3. Now, if you can- try to sense or feel an energetic band of golden light from the center of your stomach (solar plexus chakra- represents ego of you)

Step 4. Then visualize connecting that golden light to your heart chakra. This is a golden light of healing energy. The heart Chakra is located in the center of your chest.

Step 5. Now connect that same energetic golden light to your third eye which is the 6th chakra located in-between your eye brows on the front of your face.

Step 6. Connect another golden light connected from the 3rd eye to the top of your head; this is the 7th crown chakra.

This is connecting your mind to the energetic golden light –the all *knowing you* or some call it "your higher-self".

All of these points are energetically connected with a golden light.

Step 7. Imagine small arches from one point to the next. Try to feel or imagine a flow of light in this golden string of vibrations. Feel or imagine the gold vibes flowing back and forth.

All of these connected points are *"to "communicate, accept and exchange."*

This is the "human- you" connecting with the "energy of you, also known as your true soul."

I explain the *true soul* of "you "to clients being the energy of you- for an example: when a human passes into the light, passes away (deceases of life on Earth) the energy of the soul continues on. Energy is infinite.

Whether you believe your energy goes to heaven, to another dimension, or is reborn- it is the *energy of the soul that goes somewhere*. If you agree to that- it helps you understand the way energy travels. Energy is vibrations that can be in "places." As humans we cannot necessarily "see" with our human eyes. Vibrations do exist because they are a form of energy. Vibrations resonate over time and space.

Okay back to the meditation...

If you have a hard time visualizing the golden light- it is okay if you skip that part. After reading this last paragraph I think you understand the way of "connecting energy. "It was connecting the human *you* with the energy of *your essence.* Then communicating or placing "all of 'you' in sync".
Please continue...by stating:

Step 8. "I am to be of pure energy. I, (Your full name) at this time 20_ _ (year) Earth dimension-I bring only love into my pure energy;
I release all blocks- all thoughts that are *other than* the light.

I release all judgments of me and others that are *other than* the light.

Any and all habits that are other than the light- **I release and exchange with positive energy**.

Step 9. At this time specifically say what you would like to *replace* **with positive**.

It can be a thought, vision or pattern. You should feel or sense the exchange and visualize or state your specifics aloud the positive outcome. Make it something that replaces the negative you currently have.

One example would be: If I had a pattern of attracting people that take advantage of my niceness- I would allow myself to let go of that –release my pattern of attracting that into my life. I replace with attracting people that respect me and I respect them in all ways.

If you have more than one habit or pattern to release-you can do one at a time. Remember make it *your **intention*** that you truly ***change and exchange the negative patterns to be positive.***

Step 10. Once you have gone over your list- Replacing each of the negatives to positives- read and say this statement directing it at "you."

"I only see myself as pure and high vibration energy which means happy, healthy and loving.

"I only allow loving relationships in my energy."

"I only allow loving energy around me."

"I am always safe and protected by loving energies."

"I allow myself and I deserve to have only positive equal energy exchange with all beings of energies, and all that is energy, including myself.
I allow and accept these "Changes" in my life to be of goodness and advancement.
I only allow the light within, around and in my thoughts on this 20_ _ (year) Earth dimension including *all* of where I exist, existed and reside- in all *my forms* human and beyond."

Step 11. Once again take 11 deep breaths in and 11 long breaths out.
Step 12. Lastly, give gratitude to yourself and all energies of life.

To complete this soul talking with yourself-

I always advise you to drink a glass of water and place your feet flat on the floor or ground. This will bring harmony and help you feel stable after any meditation. Some people call this grounding yourself and being *back-* into your physical body.

Most people will feel great. The emotional weight is lifted from their bodies. You may feel tired, this is because you released old emotional junk from your energy field and soul energy. Take some time to relax or take a nap. This is the usual protocol after a soul talk.

Join the Happy

Now that you joined the happy segment of people in the world, it's great to share the success! Many people call and email me of their success with soul talking. They shared results of releasing old patterns from their life. They expressed they were using the soul talking directions- with positive intention and they allowed the negative to release from their energy fields. It is amazing that taking 30-60 minutes to perform a meditation can clear negative energy and bring positive results in a person's current life!

Time?

My Spirit guides say there is "no time." Humans invented a clock or measure of time. These spirit guides and Angels talk of *moments or experiences.*

The measure of time and space can only be known to those that "experience." Outside what humans know as relative space-beyond boundaries what scientists can currently calculate; there is what these Angels and spirits call "MORE."

More-you say?

Yes, more.

If you loved the Soul talk with yourself-
You will be ecstatic about *soul talking with other people!*

This is a message about this Shift in the Earth and the Universe.

Every 11 years a Shift cleanse "happens." This is an opportunity to do a total clearing of the soul.

Experiences, connections occurrence's that are not equal nor positive to be cleansed from the soul. Not only cleared from our human thoughts- but from the soul. No imprint of any old "junk"- it is gone!

This includes habits, patterns, and occurrences and or situations. Keeping the good energy and releasing the negative energy from this life- all past and/or parallel lives depending on your beliefs.   With doing a soul cleanse - only positive remains in the soul's energy imprint. This meditation, similar to the previous, brings peace between others and you.

I need to explain a few more things before you do this Soul talking meditation.

Good News

I was honored to be a part of this cleanse in my lifetime. You may have missed the current **"window"** to do this extreme cleanse. But the good news is this meditation of exchanging energy between you and other people proves powerful any time you perform it.

There will be another major cleansing window in year 2023, then 2034 that will be incredible. This includes every 11 years thereafter as well.

Don't wait

The spirit guides ask you *not to wait* for the next open window. They want you to get the benefits of this "exchange" **now**. You will feel the balance of your soul when you cleanse equally. And by all means, do it in 2023 and beyond too!

These guides expressed there will be another flow of information after year 2021- they call it "higher knowledge."

This info will be about an advanced way of healing- in addition to soul talking and what this book just explained.

Basically the Spirits messaged me that in 11 years many humans will have advanced in many ways of healing. Giving and receiving when the energy exchange is accepted and then 2021 there will be advancement.

This advancement has a name called 'The Humanitarian Light force.' This will be telepathic, endearing life among humans and those who complied in the previous "time" will be of it.

They mean in 2021 this *advanced information* will be emerging at that time. Until then, the guides want us to use these healing modalities of energy self-healing to advance. This includes soul talking and manifesting with the energy exchange. They say *spiritually channeled healing* is done by people utilizing the visually energetic Healing Mandalas, Light Tunnel Energy, utilizing Reiki energy healing and Crystal healing. This is information for humans to learn how to heal themselves.

For now we learn and advance. This is not to say you can't cleanse and advance on a physical, mental, spiritual or emotional level – you can do this anytime.

Although these specific *windows of time* are considered *the best moments to* cleanse the core of our energy, we can start soul-talking today!

In definition it means we get a deep cleansing from carrying negative or any old junk-from this life to any other lifetime or existence by soul talking.

 As I have said- depending on what your belief system is- this *cleanse* -in a certain window of time- means clearing junk from *this parallel* (Earth) to any other parallel or dimension.

Basically you are able to clear all negative stuff/energy from Earth and/or any other realm that exists. These spirit guides said this is a *gift of advancement.*

If we -as people, aka humans, "let go, clear and cleanse"- this negative energy can be replaced with even or a positive energy exchange. This is an exchange of love, light, healthy emotions and positive thoughts.

Now you know that when we have old connections that are negative- we need to release those emotions that are attached to those thoughts. Remember.

This basically means releasing the *energy* of negatives. What most people might *not* know/ *is* -we don't necessarily have to release a person from our lives. I mean you don't necessarily have to ignore them or never talk to them again.

RELATIONSHIPS WITH OTHER PEOPLE

If you made a person feel bad *or* they made you feel bad - or 'did" something negative to you or vice versa.

Or if you both hurt each other- this person or you *can* have a negative attachment. Negative attachments are vibrations that are connected to theirs and /your energy field and is held in their/your soul's imprint.

I will give an example:
If you have a family member that is continuously verbally abusive, you can cut the "cord or tie." What you are cutting is the negative emotion/energy that person "put or places" on you. You don't have to erase that person from your life to do this.

You will cut those negative emotions and thoughts from your energy field / auric bubble. You can also cut that negative emotion which is negative vibrations of energy from your true soul's energy imprint. Energy can be released *if* you ***allow it***. Know that you can have that person in your life and like or love them as "a family member or friend or simply as a human being".

When releasing any negative energy – it must always be *replaced* with positive. You replace the negative words, thoughts and/or actions, occurrences, situations or memories that the person placed on you.

If they were/are negative words or if they said them a long time ago -you can always relinquish any negative emotions at any time.

I would also like to add-if someone has passed on from Earth- you can always change the energy between you. This is because energies exist over time and space. It can be done.

First- always release the negative emotions, cut and replace with positive thoughts and words. You can also use positive actions.

Let's use a family member as an example again.

When you come face to face with that family member-you already understand they are negative towards you. Let their words and actions roll off you. Know and realize that it is ***their*** "junk" not yours- You ***don't own*** it!

Now that you know how to rid yourself of other peoples "junk"- placed on you-YOU will not let it "stick". This is because you understand **how** energy works. YOU- *allow only love and light to stick!* And that's it!

Let's say that family person was your father. He's hard to avoid. You can always love him for being your "father" or for being a human being. Most importantly -you *don't* have to allow, accept or take on *his* "negative junk." Love him for being your father. Not *his* negative actions or words he may place on you.

Remember cord cutting & releasing is incredibly empowering. But you MUST replace unwanted or negative energy with positive energy.

Empty Space- the void

I say this because once you have *"owned energy"* whether it is negative or positive or null- there is "space" there. It now needs to be filled with positive. If you rid yourself of any energy and don't replace it-that is a "void of energy."

A **void** or **empty space**- is where energy once existed. Whether positive or negative- it is gone. If you allowed it – you can *also allow letting it go.*

I like to describe it by saying if there was a "space" that was currently filled; now you released or cut it out. Energetically there is still a 'space" that exists. It is just empty or a "void of energy."

You can feel "off balance" and may go back to old ways of thinking to "fill the voided space" with "negative replacement junk."

Previously, we used the example of the family member being a negative father. It may not be the same *junk*, but you might go pick up a *significant* other that treats you the same way as the negative father did. That is filling the void NEGATIVELY. You don't want to fill the void with old junk!

Okay, I hope that was understood. **If you release- you replace**. Make it a positive replacement!

If you release a person -their actions or their negative words- you can replace any and all of it with something totally different.

Do this by replacing a negative person's energy by doing something positive for yourself. You can take yoga, start riding a bike, cook, or try a new fun class that fills that time or void. These are just some healthy lifestyle examples to fill your voids. It can balance your total being.

Why, why, why..

I strive for a positive reconstruction of the energy in and on the Earth- including atmosphere. This should be a main goal of humans to utilize the positive energy exchange.

The cosmic period of time- is *now*. Since all energy is made up of vibrations-people can change their energy by shifting and learning to adapt and live happy and healthy lives.

It just takes new ways of thinking. If we retrain our brains to bring new actions into our lives we can change.

"Talking to the souls of others-from a human being/ true soul,
to another human being/ true soul."

The soul talking with others - let's get back to that. This is an energy clearing- an energy exchange of true souls. Similar to the energy exchange with the energy of "you"- but this meditation is "your true soul's energy with another's person or animal or someone whom has passed from Earth.

With respects to those who have passed

If you have lost a friend, loved one or family member, this meaning, deceased people, please go to the directions how to soul talk with another person on the next page . You can do the technique for these circumstances:

Did the person you loved pass into the light without you saying goodbye?
Did you feel as if the person that passed is now visiting you?
Did you have an argument before they passed?
Were there unsaid words?
Do you love them dearly and just want to know they are okay?

A MEDITATION WITH YOU AND OTHERS
SOUL TALKING WITH OTHERS

If you have-had -or think you have negative energy
between you and another person or an animal this is for
you. Exchanges can be made positive- from your past
present or parallel lives.
Yep, that's YOU.

If you are human- *you* have SOMETHING TO exchange! So
Time to make a positive energy exchange between you
and them to let go & replace with positive!

**"Keep equal energy exchange and your life will complete
as clean, cleansed and clear. You will advance
continually. Harmony and balance restored within self
and the energy of 'self' as a true soul of light - energy.
Soul talk- now."**

Step 1: You sit and make a list. This list is of all the people
things occurrences, situations, experiences that you
remember as negative (hurtful to yourself, by others to

you or you to them! If you find your list is quite long, that is normal. It just means you are human!)

*Note- the people, animals or spirit energy you are making the exchange, *do not* have to be physically present. This is an energetic exchange.

Step 2: Once your list is done, you relax, breathe, and take 11 deep breaths in and 11 long exhales out. Imagine breathing in the love, exhaling the negative.

Now set a positive intention and feel that you *want and allow* this exchange to happen: say aloud or in your mind:
I, _____ _____ (Your full name. First, middle, and last name. If you have a nickname or a married name, add that too. Say all the names that are known as "you"!)
I am here to make a positive energy exchange with
_____. (The person's name or visualize their face if you don't know their name.)
You can visualize that occurrence, situation, or just place an actual picture or visualize the person (or animal) or the "energy of that situation."

State the **way *you* feel**. Then state the way ***they* made you feel.** With good Intention, Express fully of your emotions to release the energy of that situation. (Yes, you can cry, yell, be sorry, or all of the above and more.)

* Note- this process of "this cleanse" can be very intense for some people. The situations or conversations can bring up anger, fear, sorrow or serenity. Please remember the spirit guides wanted me to state that *"this soul cleanse, is not about "blame, it is about releasing and replacing energy of 2 souls for an energy exchange of the light."*

If you are serious in completing this soul talking and cleanse, you will really truly "feel" the energy exchange. That is how you know it is "working." Some people have felt it instantly during the soul talk. Many felt a sense of peace afterwards up to a few days.

Remember you can talk aloud or in the mind, this is telepathic energy which is basically the same as verbal*." Every thought is energy."*
Then, once you completed this step, continue onto:

Step 3: Ask the person or animal, basically it is the "energy "of who or what you are directing this soul talking to. (Who knows, could be a tree you cut down and felt bad about it.)

Ask the energy of those souls to <u>accept this new positive</u> energy exchange of *light to replace the negative energy* that existed. Don't worry; you don't have to" hear "anything back, if you do- great. If not, keep going, it is still positive energy going out to that particular soul of that person...Please also note that if this energy is between a soul that has passed, a person whom has deceased in a

human body, you can still "soul talk" to them.
You can make the energy positive no matter where they
are *"over space and time, energy is on all dimensions and
all levels; it exists "everywhere."*

During this exchange, *feel or sense* the emotions of love,
solace and peace. Strongly visualize or feel the energy of
forgiveness or understanding in your heart chakra (the
center of your chest)- when you sense this- feel a pull in
the exchanged energy to you and know they have also
received the positive energy into their existence-into their
energy of their soul. The guides say: *"when humans "look
through others eyes, all can be resolved."*

*Note - when I personally did step 3, I visualized and drew
a heart on a piece of paper and pretended I handed it to
that person across from me and visualized in my mind that
they accepted it and I then felt this amazing sensation over
my heart and chest area, it then traveled through my
entire body. It was amazing.*

Step 4: Close out the conversation of energy by thanking
them and give gratitude for this opportunity with them to
make amends and state that *"both of your true souls have
made an even and Positive energy exchange to be equal".*
Say your goodbyes and Breathe in and out fully for 11
breaths.

Step 5: Congratulations are in order! Know that you are

successful in the exchange. Know that you deserve this positive energy as they do too.
Take a break and do a few more on your list, if any.

You are on your way to *"advancement of a true soul."* You will notice in the next few days a *"change"* in your energy, the guides say: *"humans will feel lighter-peaceful."*

Wonderful news

I have received many emails from people all over the world doing the soul talking & energy exchanges.

Many people shared their amazing soul talk results. Some stories were very extremes cases.
One woman hadn't heard from her father in years. One week after the meditation he called her on the phone! Out of the blue (ya think?).

They had a nice conversation that was not of the norm from him. It was nice- the woman was happy just to hear from her estranged father-let alone him being nice to her.

Another story- A woman from Florida emailed me; she received an omen from an animal guide that let her know her son was in the light. He had passed 1 year prior. She was soul talking to him a night previous to receiving her omen. She told me she felt he was now in a good place-at peace.

 So many people have shared their positive exchanges. They felt they had shifted into a better place in their lives. I am glad they shared the information- gratitude. If you want to share your experience please email me.

What are entitlement issues?

Chapter 8

Entitlement or Energy Exchange?

If someone gives you something, whether it is a book to borrow or a smile- do you automatically think –"what does that person want from me?"

Have you ever "expected" another person to give you something if you gave them something?

I am not talking about a purchase at a store. That is a different story. I am talking about the *thought* of *thinking* that if you want something you intentionally "think" that you deserve something in return. I'm saying -other than the words of "thank you as a return of energy.
The world is a funny place, well at least on Earth. I notice every day in conversations that most people do assume that if you do something or offer a favor-the other person feels indebted to give you something physically back of the same value.

Is that an energy exchange?

Yes- it is.
 But- is it a positive energy exchange?
 When we *expect someone* to give us something only because you are giving to them is not.

 No. That is not a positive *intention* with the energy exchange.

A positive energy exchange is when I *offer* you something- let's say a tangible object, and let's say that tangible object is cookies.

I bought chocolate cookies and I am offering you one to eat or take some. I do this without thinking you owe me- or thinking next time *you* have food or something that you owe me.

The gesture was innocent. Unfortunately, TV and our society reaks in promoting that we have to *give to get.* *Society trains us and makes us think that* "I will only do something to help you if you do something for me." This is a selfish way of existence.

A positive energy exchange is a smile; I smile at you, you at me. I want to offer you a cookie; you say "thanks." No agenda, no debt.

There's a reason we gave that word, "debt" a bad connotation... "Debt "it means "owes" the word intrinsically sounds negative or bad.

The good or positive energy exchange has the intention that is thoughtless or simply kind, or lighthearted, not expectant or preplanned in the way of wanting return value. It is hard today because it is automatic with most of us. It happened to me and I fell into it.

I owned a wedding flower business years ago. I only received referrals from larger companies such as hotels and party planners if I gave them a kick back (money).

I was rated #1 in my area for my expertise, but they only sent me business if I slipped them money without "other" people at their establishment knowing.

After 18 years in that business, I was disgusted at myself for paying some of them and disgusted because I was part of that negative exchange. It made me feel yucky and used. The point that only with the exchange of monies – I was able to "work" at those specific venues. It made me feel like all my hard work was irrelevant. I am thankful however; all my brides were thankful. Witnessing their happiness on the day of their marriage made up for the other negative exchanges.

During my "flower days" my best way of gaining business was word of mouth. I provided all of my brides with the best service and products. I love flowers and that industry, but that one part of it- I could do without.

Although I was successful, I felt the energy exchange between those particular people (discerning.) I decided I wasn't going to "play that game." I found I felt so much happier in my work.

Today I'm a proprietor of a Mindful healing center. Very few people come to "play that negative exchange." Most people come with whole hearts. The exchanges are true and simple- as it should be. In the past, people traded. People gave or received services and products by honoring themselves and others. Happy to do the best they could at their jobs. That is true kindness without entitlement.

Take time to notice yourself and people around you. Try to make the energy between you and others positive. Stop that mindless process of over thinking, make a kind gesture and let go of "expecting." Life is much easier this way.

A few messages you may find interesting.
Messages from: Archangel Michael, The Spirits of the Light, The Light Ones, St. Germain and a spirit master called EROM.

"Energy cannot be duplicated. That is why a soul is original. You cannot copy a soul. This is the same with the energy of a soul. An example would be an energy healer- they channel energies of the light-through their soul and human casing (body). This brings the energy uniqueness that no other can duplicate.

This is the reason humans are attracted to other humans in several ways- not only human traits such as personality and looks, but soul traits that are unique energies. Energy of the soul is what another soul senses, feels as human or non-human and is attracted to. High vibrations of the soul core cannot be duplicated.

Humans found a way to duplicate vibrations of sounds- but not soul energies. It will never be done. Cloning is not cloning of a soul, only its structure (body)."

Energies such as entities have auras like we have auras. They too have electromagnetic fields which can be sensed on Earth. If a spirit is on this dimension their aura or electromagnetic field can be felt by some sensitive humans. Sensitive people are sometimes called psychics, empaths, mediums or intuitives.

Here is an example: I channel messages for many people- Sometimes my clients ask me about feeling energies of spirit guides. They express that sometimes they "sense a presence- that feels dark." They want to know if that presence or spirit they felt is there to harm them since it felt scary to them.

I ask these clients: "Does the *energy* that surrounds you feel negative?" They answer, "yes."

Basically what is happening- whatever spirit or entity is present *is* in their auric field. The entity most likely projected energy that is letting them know that it doesn't want you in that space. It can be for many reasons. One common reason is that the entity may have been human and passed away suddenly. At the moment of life ending- the person became in spirit form- and didn't realize they were no longer in human form. This could keep them on the Earth dimension. No one can see them, and they see you in their home or space.

I would be angry too. What I'm getting at is that this entity is mad. This can make your aura feel uneasy or sense that same emotion, "mad."

If they are in your auric field feeling mad - you can feel or sense this emotion because your aura and this (spirit's energy) aura are in touch with yours.

That is how you sense it, the presence of this ghost, deceased person. It is also true when you sense a loving spirit, deceased or angel; you feel a good emotion or sensations, and some even see "light, or figures of light.

Those who are very sensitive and visual can actually see an angel or entity. They can decipher if it is a good or bad feeling on an energetic level. All in all, this is how we can sense these energies through our auric energies, our auric fields. They are like our fingerprints -they can identify ourselves and others. I also explain them to be patterns of energy which are basically vibrations that we feel as emotions.

Chapter 9

Empathetic abilities – sensitive peeps

I have a client that comes often to receive energy healings. Every week she comes and says she's always confused and feels bad. Sometimes it's emotional, sometimes physical. She currently sees an herbalist, a counselor, an acupuncturist and me for energy healing and channeling. On the 3rd month, I had seen progress. I watched her interactions with others and at first I thought she just needed attention, whether it was from her talking of her unknown illnesses or for getting involved with other people's lives perhaps because she was lonely at this time in her life.

Then after a day or two later she had a channeling session with the angel Archangel Michael and me as a conduit. I channeled the message to her-he said "you are an empath."
Now we already established this when she first started coming but, this is what he said to her next" you constantly pick up co-workers, friend, neighbors, just anyone you talk to or pass, you pick up their energies."

I knew exactly what he was saying. He went on to say you never let go of these, physically or emotionally." You don't know how *you* feel because you are feeling other's pains and emotions -whether happy or sad or aches etc., you are confused. Anyone would be- you cannot feel YOU."

My client's eyes lit up as mine did, it totally made sense. All these doctors she was seeing, even the herbalist, said I can't find anything I don't know why you feel like you do. Every day she thought she had some different ailment, a knee pain, and stomach ache, then emotional trauma.

It was a light that went off, we _realized_ all these were the people she was surrounded by and not only that, she would pick up emotions from reading a book that had expressed dangers and abnormal behaviors which she took on as her own!

I am also an empath. I was self-taught to first identify where the emotion or pain is coming from, and once I establish that it is not mine, I immediately let go of this emotion or physical pain. I only keep the happy feelings lol.
I told my client how she can "release anything that is other than the light," meaning anything that is not good from anyone or any entity, a book, TV you name it.

I taught her to know "if it's not yours- don't own it!" She learned how to trust herself in doing so. I gave her this scenario, if she <u>didn't</u> bump her toe and her toe does hurt, it most likely is **not** her pain to bear. There was no self-_cause_ of the pain.

She empathically picked up that the cause of her painful

toe was from someone who was having pain in *their* toe. She was sensing this energetically from the other person's toe pain. She was simply *absorbing* the negative emotion and physical pain from the other person's auric energy.

She realized she was standing next to person that had a "toe injury" at that time. She learned *to identify and realize, then allowed herself let go of a negative* that was not hers to own-energetically speaking.

Today she is fine and feels great, no need for countless doctors. She is maintaining her health and is very happy instead of confused. She knows how and what *she* feels today and every day. What a relief for her!
Thank you, Archangel Michael!

"Change is good- learn more about you.
Only you can change you.

Be your best. Allow change, allow advancement."

 A worldly view about the Energy Exchanges with the Earth and the atmosphere: *The dimensions are getting thicker, due to the energy exchange in the atmosphere, the planets are moving and other dimensions are feeling this as we are on Earth. The change or part of the new 2nd shift is nearing. As we*

spoke there are many changes affecting the Earth within the tectonic plates and also with the air changing.

This means the Earth has changes. We will notice the changes to be positive or negative. The hope is to make our perception of "change' to be positive.

The change overall is letting sensitive people on Earth feel this and know the changes are coming soon. Our human bodies can sense it and want to adapt.

Early humans learned to adapt to weather conditions (and more). We know we will have the same evolution of adapting to the new air and the new way of life. The atmosphere is changing from planets and planetary destruction, meaning that many planets are affected by our Earth. Earth has been, as I say, sabotaged due to human inadequacies, but also because its structure has been compromised. Humans "moved" too many sections or parts of the Earth and for this along with the planetary pulls will start as it already has in the first shift and will continue to self-destruct piece by piece from above the Earth and below the Earth until it has been renewed".

Why the atmosphere is changing, meaning frequencies-vibrations

Everything affects everything on all dimensions. We are all energies that occupy the universes and beyond. Each should be responsible for what is happening. All of the cell towers, smart meters on our homes and each of us having several devices that emit frequencies that can be positive or negative are covering our atmosphere. All which can affect the Earth's electromagnetic fields and our individual auras/electromagnetic fields. These are vibrational differences that are felt. Mainly, people are becoming more sensitive and or intuitive due to the human aura being more permeable from nonstop, viable frequencies.

In the future other entities will come to teach us how to adapt to this new Earth. Occurrence by occurrence we will change. We will have to adapt.

We can teach the young people to learn skills that can help them to communicate with other life beings on other dimensions. We also should teach the young to communicate properly with other people in their lives on Earth.

These same light beings are currently teaching people in the world we know as Earth to communicate and adapt to changes. They teach us the movement of energy-vibrations and frequencies. The purpose is for people to advance to a higher frequency to live in happier loving communities. These light beings want to get our attention. They want to shake us up. They want to get us going - using the positive or equal energy exchanges in our lives. Every exchange emits or holds a vibration.

In short, we need to be happy, live happily and be good to the Earth and each other. This *will make positive changes* in all worlds that exist.

"Let your high vibrational energy emit to be of the Light"

I was advised to share a channeled message about the numbers 11-11-11. They said this was a strong message that needs to be heard and realized over and over and over again! In the numerology I was taught by spirit guides, they say the number 11 means making a decision, right from wrong. Many of us see the numbers doubled or tripled and *we noticed-* this means
you are mindful. It also is for you to realize what decision you need to make at that moment you saw the numbers appear.

This message of 11-11-11 said:
"As the shift continues of the need for humans to work together to keep vibrations high, also meaning happiness, in their emotions other than negative emotions which bring low vibrational energies that will surround the atmosphere and result in movement of the planetary world."

This is a healing-it will progress. The planetary shift is here- you will feel more changes- we know you have felt many changes already in the last couple years- as you have written, it will be the truth- prepare-spread the word of the new world to come adaptation to new air-of dimensional changes all of us alike will adapt. To listen to our guidance as it will be of the light and is needed greatly for healing to come all humans, all-life, planets, atmospheres together life force exists and will continue in other forms.

We see that each human has individual needs. You will find that "healing work" you do will increase of the number of humans meaning they will increase in needing alternative light energies to adapt, survive and carry existence, survival is known to humankind. It will always exist. We share guidance to redeem the light as many misconstrue the messages as dark- we are only here in light and love to create, preserve and inherently show force of energy surround Earth and humans as vibrational pull of the atmosphere is and will change as told to you in 2021. It has started. Be well -we will guide you as needed. Amen-"

Sure sounds like we all can make a conscious decision on that.

What do numbers mean?
The relationship with the numbers 1 and 11

Since the numbers 11-11 always seem to be "noticed" for me and millions of others around the globe, I would like to share that sequential numbers are quite common in many of us. Seeing sequential numbers can give us great insight on what is going on in our life.

I have been working with numbers to see what they mean to us on Earth. Spirit guides have confirmed that the number 11 means "making a decision, good from bad, right from wrong. " If you see doubles of the number 11 it is intensified. This meaning, "I really need to make that decision sooner!" Because it has been noticed repeatedly-you are taking longer than it should to make that important decision.

If you see a number 1 , that means "letting go, let life flow, also taking charge of one's life to bring more loving energy into it." The spirits stated "you have to recharge yourself with positive energy after you let go."

Numbers can represent many insights. Some people see sequential numbers such as 1234. This can be telling you to "get things in order!"

But the doubled or tripled numbers seem to be more predominant and present a clearer "message." As I mentioned above, notice how you are feeling or what you were thinking about when you notice the numbers. That's the real clue to connecting the *message* with the numbers.

Ponder this....

Chapter 10

Energy exchange with Angels & Spirits/Universes and Parallel Exchanges

It's important if you want to "communicate with Angels or spirits that you have good intentions. It is especially important that you _do not have_ "distorted" energy. My description of "distorted energy" is someone who is abusing their body, mainly the function of the human brain. Yes, this means a glass of wine, a toke, trippin' or anything remotely close. All of these "things" distort energy. It distorts your energy in a way that brings insecurities, fear and can also make telepathic communication or "visual messages from the "mind's eye" _inaccurate_ to say the least!

Some people that can sense or see auras of humans can feel or see the electromagnetic field that surrounds our human bodies. These readers of auras can "see" or sense a grey, icky yuck around a person who has 'distorted' their energy field.

With this said, when conversing, telepathically to a spirit guide or Angel your information will most likely be 'heard wrong." Many times an angel won't visit; they will stay away rather than having you interpret the information and guidance in a misconstrued manner.

If you are a person who uses 'tools' such as pendulums, oracle card decks for guidance or readings, my suggestion is make sure you are not under the 'influence." This distorted energy is considered dirty because most people who use drugs or alcohol can be holding a lower vibration due to insecurities of themselves or of life in those moments of usage. This can be why if you are trying to use an oracle deck or pendulum to do a self-reading and you don't believe or trust the answer or message you received. You may find yourself saying: "My message wasn't clear and I didn't feel like it is accurate!"

This is not to be down on having some fun. But to me, would you ask a doctor to perform a surgery on you if he's drunk? You have to feel what is true to yourself; trust is a main part of receiving information from spirits and angels. This is also my reasoning about going to a healing center for an energy healing session; would you want a healer to have distorted energy flowing in your energy field?

This is a "no no" with the Angels and spirit guides. *"Stay of pure energy to receive the pure accurate messages of the light.* " A message straight from the Angels themselves. They wanted this quote in this book.

To make an equal energy exchange with Angels or spirits guides, it's quite simply put in this message*" We will help you, if you ask us accurately and with loving intentions for all involved, without ego and pure, clean energy."*

That is how they would like to "exchange" with us as humans.

Universes and parallels

This is a concept of the energy exchange can be a bit confusing since the information given about parallels and universes existing other than Earth can be hard to grasp.

The exchanges between them as I was told (yes again by angel and spirits) that all of us exist with **"different time and space" energy is still the same, it is powerful and great, but to exchange purity it is best to be accepted as even or positive."**

I have learned from my career with energy healing and reading as a conduit, that many of us have instances or situations that we "feel" that we have had, but not always sure it was from this life. As we grow and live, we 'sense "these occurrences or situations to be a "lesson."

Lessons move us out of one part of our life or our life's view- and *into new* ways of "seeing or experiencing" life. I strongly feel this is happening as our energy of our existence can be in more than one place at a time.

Our dreams and thoughts along with déjà vu can make most of us think more deeply about our lives. About how, why and where we can be and what we learn on a human, Earthly, day- to- day basis.

The notion of past lives or parallels is intriguing since it is hard to prove, but easy to believe.
Each of us decides for ourselves until those "coincidences happen" and can *change* our minds or help us realize that "energy" can travel.

Energy waves are kind of like cell phones. We cannot see them but they travel and exist. Because we have flesh and bones our bodies make us grounded to Earth, but our, minds, thoughts and true soul of energy can travel to distance places. After all, they are just vibrations.

For me and many other people, these "travels" seem very real in meditations, sleeping or hypnosis. How can so many people make this stuff up? Especially when visions have so much detail, how can it be proven? Details come through about a lot of places on Earth that currently exist but when locations where I have never been appear along with seeing people's faces I never knew, that's amazing.

Some visions or travels of the mind's energy is proof to me that we can connect with unknown "places" that don't seem to be of this planet Earth but beyond.

The energy exchanges we can have with other realms, dimension, parallels or past lives (if ya believe in that) to me are relevant in proving that energy is "energy." Energy vibrations travel through space and time. Meaning everything that exists in my mind as visions or experiences or maybe they are just dreams- they are all energy vibrations transmitted by or to me somehow.

To exchange a thought or dream that energy exists and is amazing to evaluate. In my personal experiences and my client's experiences these are "lessons or learning sessions" within our mind's travels. We have experienced places that are possibly other than our conscious living-this is proof enough that a positive exchange is pertinent there-in our mind's travels too.

One revelation on parallels is that our human body can be on Earth dimension, but our energy body and mind can be on another at the same moment. This is called a parallel dimension.

Is this what absent minded "is?"

One of my examples: Have you ever misplaced an item? Let say your glasses. You know you placed them on the table by the door, but now they aren't there in that spot. You may have asked others "have you seen my glasses, I know I put them there on that table?" They reply, "No haven't seen, em." Then five hours later they are in that spot you originally thought you placed them.

No-really you aren't as disorganized as you thought- or were you temporarily in a parallel? People have used the old expression "are you *absent minded*?" I like that expression; most old sayings are somewhat true. My notion: You *were* in the *same place* but a parallel of that same place in between a moment. I know it sounds tricky, but it's truly plausible.

Maybe that's where the old expression "precious moments" came from????

Remember, if you
"Look through other's eyes, the world will be exchanged as proper liking to all."

BONUS

Do ya want to learn how to manifest with equal energy in detail?   Do read on…

Chapter 11

Techniques How to Manifest with equal Energy
Exchange. Love/Relationships, Job, Tangible stuff,
Knowledge and Self-Realization

Manifesting
with the Equal Energy Exchange

How would you like to receive all that you desire?

I am sure you have heard of "affirmations." That is when
you verbally repeat something you want in your life.
Another way is to pray for what you want. That is, of
course, if you believe in other sources that are mightier
than humans.

I realized if I want to receive what I want or desire,
whether I ask the Universe, pray to Angels or higher
sources, that it is possible. I believe all of us can ask and
manifest what we want. However, I was clairaudiently
taught by these higher beings that "asking" must be done
with equal energy exchange."

What *is* Equal energy? What do I mean that I was told?

First of all, a person that can sense vibrational messages

through hearing is a clairaudient. You probably heard of a clairvoyant. That's more common.

A clairvoyant can see, hear, feel, and smell, basically using all their senses to receive messages or information. It also is identifying vibrations which is energy on a different level than most humans can relate to. This information comes from sources other than human or from another realm, dimension, parallel or all of the above.

In my case, I sense and hear these messages. As a clairaudient person I can do this. I describe it like tuning in, similar to a radio. I am able to tune- in on a frequency that comes from Archangels and other high beings. I can hear specific messages and can communicate with these Angels and Spirits. I know this may sound kooky to some non-believers of the psychic phenomena, but it's true.

Equal energy exchange was explained to me by these higher spirits of knowledge as I wrote in the previous pages. They told me that humans have not been "asking" the correct way to manifest what they want, need or desire. I showed you briefly in the 10 things you should know section of the book. But the details are the key to success with manifesting.

We all know there are tons of books that you can read about how to manifest what you want. Not one book explains it with equal energy.

These Angel guides laughed about this as I communicated with them. They said to me: *"Wow, we made things so simple. You and your human friends constantly make life on Earth dimension difficult for themselves. Don't they know we are here to help them and all they have to do is Ask correctly?"* I agreed. I replied "we humans" do complicate everything. It seems we don't take time to see or feel without being rushed!

I like to use the example of how we humans work so much, (well, most of us) and we forget to take time for ourselves to breathe. I mean literally take long deep breaths in and out! It sounds silly, but think about the last time you really took a long deep breath in and out. Unless you are a Yogi, most of us don't do this or think about doing it.

I asked the Angels to educate me. They said, *Yes. We will and would you please share this information with other humans.* I said sure.

The Task
My task is to teach everyone how to: manifest what you want and desire with equal energy exchange.
After I wrote that last line, I felt like there was cool music playing, similar to the theme of Star Wars or the big bang theory...must be in my head. Or the spirit guides are messin' with me again..lol

I am making it simple to manifest, as I was specifically advised by the higher educated beings and Angels.

Basically, all those energies of the light (positive energy) that want "us humans" to succeed and be happier in our lives on Earth gave me the 101 on manifesting.

The guides joke a lot with me when they said: *"Humans create their own chaos. They have to realize what they want, before asking and manifesting."*

Maybe they weren't joking. I guess it's up to us "humans" to figure out *what we want and need*, **then** manifest it! No wishy –washy asking. Be direct, detailed and clear.

On the next pages, I wrote how to specifically "manifest." You can follow the guidelines and of course you can add what you like or take out some things to your preference. You might want to grab a notebook and pen to figure out what you want, and then choose what your goals are to start.

Please remember the most important part **DO NOT take out- the equal exchange!** That was a message I just heard from the Angels. They made me write that bold and big in the book.

Oh, the Angels just told me that some of you reading this part of the book and are saying in your heads: *who am I to ask such high spirits like Angels or God to help me?*

This is the Angel's answer (I heard it loud and clear*): We allow you to ask for what you want. It is not being selfish. Only when you ask without the equal exchange you will feel selfish. Understand that all people deserve good things in life. That includes you! The purpose for all of life to use*

*this equal energy exchange is to balance the worlds, Earth
and beyond. All humans affect each other. All humans
affect the Earth. All of Earth affects our Universes.*
That was clear enough for me. Of course if you did not
include the energy exchange in your manifest it would be a
me, *me, me* selfish request.

The Angels also want to express the following directions
when you start to manifest: *"Make sure when you take the
moment to ask us for what it is you need, that you are
specific as possible. WE get a lot of requests here and we
need to help you the best we can, be specific on all asking,
give us "your time-moment and location" by stating a
month and year also a place. We want to bring what is
needed.*

*"*There is *no time* where they are. The Angels explained to
me they use the term moment. We humans invented the
clock. They said they can get as close as they can , to our
"time" as to their "moment" to bring us opportunities and
what we are asking to come into our lives on Earth.

*"There is much importance in you stating your true desire,
your intention, and knowing you deserve what you are
asking for. Remember, every thought you have during,
before and after "asking" is energy, so make the human
thought of what it "is"-to be positive."*

Okay I'm butting in for a bit. The Angels are trying to
explain that everything we say, meaning if it is our voice or
our thought in our head, is energy.

When doing your manifesting, if you say in your head or aloud, what you wanted and afterwards you think or you use the expression "if it's meant to be -it will happen, or maybe it will come true." That is a big a no, no! You then instantly negated what you asked for by 1) Not believing it would happen, 2) placing uncertain energy which is negative or null.

That means you just wasted your time! The manifest message was distorted and won't get to them.

No Fear

What am I talking about? No fear? What does that have to do with manifesting?   It has a lot to do with it. I noticed many of my clients fear to be alone or fear of not be able to make enough money etc. If you place fear on your manifesting- that is placing negative vibrations with it- you know what that means- I hope by now you do!

It means the energy you are sending out is #1 uncertain and #2 it is lower frequency. This will not bring you what you need want or desire. Lose the fear! Be confident and know it will happen if you put the effort in the energy you send out.

Here is another tid-bit of information to make your manifesting optimal. Many people seem to obsess when they start manifesting. I have had numerous clients – more than I can count-are quite determined to manifest everything they want. This is great. But, they seem to think if they say their whole manifest script 10 times a day or more than once a week- they can make everything happen sooner. This is obsession. Obsessing is negative and fear based. The idea is positive energy brings positive energy- keep the balance- keep the energy exchange.

Please *just* follow the directions for manifesting. Manifest once a week with true intention. Know it will happen. Trust and believe.

Positive please

Use only positive words and make sure you intend on receiving what you are asking. You deserve good things in your life!

I want to clarify; I do suggest manifesting good tangible things in life but also good people or relationships. You will know what I mean by the outlined, very detailed examples. I made these tailored for you to follow. I actually wrote each of them so there's no way you will self-sabotage it. My wording is mint, straight from Archangel Michael!

Okay let the manifesting begin.

Wait. One more thing. The Angels just spoke to me and said, *and "Tell humans to only repeat their manifest once a week-their time! Otherwise, they will just be saying words without truly "feeling it, the desire of it will be lost, if they over ask- and the intent will be gone." Manifest* once a week only, please.

Sometimes I think the Angels may be saying that because they do get a humongous amount of requests and hearing them over and over must drive them crazy! Just kidding, that was just a "Jolie thought" of humor.

Seriously, if you say something over and over, it is just words that don't mean shizzle. If you are taking the time and effort, do it all the way-correctly! *Feel it, when you think it.*

Manifest

Go for it:
First make a list of everything you desire in life. It can be a loving relationship, happiness, better job or new one, a puppy or money to pay the bills. Make a list of what you want or need. This will help you find your "voids" in life. Then you can best manifest to fill the voids with positive people, things or thoughts.

* Note: I want to explain that we all look at situations in a different way than others. If you use the word "happy" to describe something or someone, happy *to you* can have a different meaning than "happy" to me. This is most likely due to how we were taught. So be more specific, if you use the word "happy, "make it detailed for example "happy emotionally" or happy because they are secure in their life, this can mean monetarily or of sound mind. Be

specific!

Below are examples for you to follow and understand the equal energy exchange way of asking.

Tip: If you want to manifest more than one job, person, item knowledge, etc... You can manifest all- but do them separately. You can have 5 things you manifest- so you would say 5 different manifesting scripts. You can say each one- once a week.

1) Manifesting a "Good Match," relationship. YES, this *is* the most popular!
   2) Manifesting a job
   3) Manifesting stuff (tangible items)
   4) Manifesting knowledge & receiving self-realization- (this can also be used to manifest how to change your thought process to be more positive.)
   5) Manifesting Money $

Manifesting a "Good Match"

Since this *is* the most popular, many of you may want to know the difference between the term *"soul mate and good match."*

The term *soul mate* is used by many people. The spirit guides find it funny- because they say "we are all souls that live together." I believe this to be true. I loved this statement so much I use it as the tag line on all my books and media.

The Angels explained- we as humans are all "souls" that currently reside on *Earth* at the same moment as other human-beings – therefore making all humans soul "mates."

All souls have many "soul mates" in a lifetime. Such a large amount – it is everyone! This definition of the word *"mates "*-means friendship and love. We can have many soul mates in one lifetime. Ultimately, **we _are all one_**. All related in some way shape or form.

Basically, all of us are soul mates to everyone –all beings- because we are all made of energy. Your mother, brother, sister, your boyfriend, girlfriend, wife, husband are all soul mates.

The definition

A **"good match"** is a person that is equal to you for a loving relationship. I understand no-one is perfect. A "good match" is one that is best for you. A *match* -that will best suit you- in this life. You are to them as they are to you. You both love each other equally. You trust each other and have similar "normal." Or you can understand each other's "normal." Think about it. You cannot be someone's good match if they aren't yours, or the relationship wouldn't last long or would not be an equally happy, positive one. It just makes sense.

What's _My_ Normal?

When I say 'normal'- I mean what you are used to in life. What you accept.

I can use this example: let's say you grow up in a family that is very caring *vs.* a family that does not show much expression. The caring *is* normal to you; you are comfortable with that interaction.

The family with less expression to each other has a normal of maybe not talking as much about their feelings to each other. Therefore these two families have different *normals*. Not one is better or worse than another- no right or wrong, just different.

If you accept someone's "normal" although it may different than your' normal'- the relationship can work. I also want to add that some people in a family don't accept the normal they grew up in or with. Some people decide or "choose" to change that "normal." As they grow old enough- or then at that time decide to change what *their normal was* or *adapt a new normal.*

Very important in a relationship

I am explaining that you can choose to *accept and allow a normal.*

If you do not accept and allow your mate's "normal", you are not considered a good match for each other.

This is not about being "perfect" or 'perfect for each other. It is the *differences* that make a wonderful relationship. This *is* saying what you *want and allow and like in your relationship can become your normal together if you choose to.*

To *find* your "good match" entails a strong, loving relationship with equal energy exchange. This is described as the "core" of what you want and allow as your "normal'. The *core* is having these main similar values: monogamy or an agreement of sexual relations, trust, respect, attraction to each other physically, mentally, emotionally. The **core** is something that serves as structure for a relationship- the strength. I use the term *core* because that is an important part of a lasting relationship. An example of a good core would be a person that knows and values the same meanings of the words: respect, honesty, honor, love and devotion. This core structure is the long standing part. We all make mistakes time to time, but if the core structure is present in the relationship- it's a match.

This is including agreeable and allowable "normals." Remember, when I say the word normal –it is the *normal* seen through **what you believe _is normal_**. Not what I -or anyone else thinks as an acceptable normal.

After all this would be **_"your good match_."** _You_ would have to live, marry or have relations with them!

The Process

Before you meet your *good match* most people will go through a process of what is called *"getting balanced."* This process has a **focus** or **transition** person or persons that come into your life. This usually (almost always) happens first- *before* you meet the **"good match."**

There can be several "focus" and transition relationships that give you "practice." Practice is before you meet your

good match. The reason for this "practicing" is that you will be truly "you" as you meet the good match.
The focus person is one who makes you have those feelings of love- butterflies in the stomach. You get that excitement to see or bump into them. They make you feel alive!

Most of the time, the *focus person* is simply that "hottie" you see at the gym or a person you see when you get your coffee. It could also be the UPS delivery person. Sometimes this focus person makes you a bit nervous. Sometimes it's just their presence that helps you take more time to care better for yourself. You know what I'm talking about -to look *extra good* when you will be walking their way. Sometimes you will have conversations with this hottie, focus person- but most of the time a *focus person* is only eye candy.

 Then **the transition** people come. You may have one or many. I have had clients that met and had relations with 14 transition people *before* their *good match*!
 The reasoning for the transition people is for you to learn how to balance yourself.

 It's you-learning about *you.* It is not about what you don't want in the other person. It is a lesson- or lessons for you to understand yourself.

This part of the process is the Angels teaching us how to build and balance our selves. To be the real *you* and build confidence. It is also for you to have more *new* experiences-experiences that you may not have had without a transition person.

Transition people are those that fill your voids of energy temporarily. You also fill their void. It is a good energy exchange-*temporarily*. It's a positive process.

Some transition relationships can be one date or a relationship of 7 months or longer together. You learn and you have fun. Then, when you aren't happy anymore together- hopefully you realize it is now time to end it, in a friendly way.

When it's time to go separate ways-make it fair to both of you. After all- you both helped each other and you *both* learned more about yourselves.

The spirit guides said to *me* **"humans make life so complicated- humans let too many emotions take over and ruin good experiences. Humans refuse at times -to let go –including when they know in their heart's it's time to move on. They let fear take over instead of being grateful of the moments and lessons were spent as good."**

Don't jump

This is because most of *us humans* are afraid of change or to be alone. Many people *jump* from one relationship to another without understanding why it is not healthy. Jumping doesn't give you time to be balanced and feel good. I can describe it as wholeness- a true balance of knowing who you are – accepting yourself and what you want or aspire in this particular time in your life. When you jump from one relationship to another- you can't realize what you want or *who you are*. It is *knowing and realizing* your identity.

If you are worried about being alone temporarily- I can advise you – you are never alone! Your Angels and spirit guides are always around if you need them and sometimes when you don't – they watch over you. I know you really want human connection as a relationship- so understand only you choose if you are alone.

Be You

I am just suggesting taking a break and getting to know yourself- and other people before you go jumping into another relationship. Especially before the last one was over!

Jumping is a pattern you can release if you choose to...FYI. If this is you- go *soul talk* with yourself!

As far as *relationships with transitional people* in our lives- the most important lesson is to have fun when "practicing." It's about new, exciting moments with someone new.

I love to give this example to my client's about how great *transition people* are.

If a super-hot guy/or gal asks you out, and wants to take you to Indian food and had 2nd thoughts because you think you hate Indian food- but you decide to go anyway because *he/she* wants to take you to their favorite place & he/she is HOT. You order a dish they suggest and realize that "hey! You love this Indian food! The man/woman may be hot and not so intelligent, but you really liked that

Indian dish! At this time in your life you learned that you currently like Indian food.

You learned about *yourself*, you had a decent time and if they weren't necessarily for you for a relationship, but you still made a friend. Ya never know they might have another friend that is just your type or vice versa. Do ya get what I'm explaining to you?   Please say, YES.

Perception

You can have fun on any date *if you choose* to have a positive outlook. If you don't add pressure analyzing each date you go on by judging them. Just be you and have a good time, relax the over thinking. Enjoy transitional people. Don't over expect – and you won't be disappointed!

Once you have had some transition relationships you know more about yourself. You will feel great, renewed and balanced. Then, when you meet your *good match*-you are in the right state of mind.

Don't pretend- The facade

All of these steps in life occur so humans can learn patience and self-realization. This includes not "making" another human into something they are not -nor should you pretend to be something you are not. Just simply be YOU! If you want to love and be loved- manifest and get out there! Don't pretend to be in love –because you *are in love with being in love. You can hurt someone, remember everyone matters.* Respect you and them, honor you and them.

Honor is being worthy and loved. Honor thyself and others.

Can I have more than one good match in my lifetime?

Yes. You can have more than one *good match* in a lifetime on Earth. Once you truly know the definition of a good match- you will know how many you had or have to date. Some people have one. Others may have had 3. Understand that these *good match* relationships have or had an equal energy exchange. These relationships are called a "good match, "according to the Angels.

Will I have contentment in my life?
Contentment comes with learning to want less and expect nothing. Knowing and understanding that happiness **comes** from *your energy.*

"Positive breeds positive"

When you glow with positive energy - others are and will be attracted to you. No-one likes to be around a negative complainer – its draining to other people. Everyone likes to hear good conversations and be around positive and inspiring energy.

Ask Now
The angels want you to manifest. Make sure you add details of what you would want. Say this manifesting only once a week. Otherwise, you are just repeating "words"

and the manifest doesn't have the same intent and feeling to make it strong and heard loudly. Concentrate. If this *is* Important to you- make time to do it correctly!

Manifesting a "Good Match"

Take 3 long breaths in and 3 exhales out. Do this at your own pace. Sit in a place you feel comfortable and peaceful, indoors or outdoors.
Try to *feel* in your heart. Focus by holding your hands lightly over your chest area. You can do this with both your hands. Now understand that your body and mind are now connected.

Continue with your focus on "Asking equally" to manifest your good match.

You can state this aloud or within. If you need to stop and get a paper and pen to write or add more details-please do this. Make your manifesting accordingly.
Please use this outline:

 I am and I allow myself to meet a _____(say man or woman, you don't need a name)
 that has healthy habits, that is respectful to me and I to them. They are attracted to me sexually, intellectually, physically and emotionally and I to them. We love each

other 100%; we are monogamous to each other (if that's what you want). We communicate properly and nicely to each other, we understand each other's feelings and way of thinking. We are both available without attachments' to meet each other and fall in love. We accept each other's "normal", we are happy together forever (or as long as you would like) and trust each other forever (how long is forever to you?). We are each other's good match and we deserve each other. We meet __ __ (insert a month and year) Earth dimension.

Options to insert if you choose, you may also add what *you* desire of your "good match."
They have a good paying job. They earn or have the amount you desire of dollars *or more.*
They are humorous and/or witty
They have values similar to yours or values you admire.
State that your families are amicable or get along positively.
You both have the same definition and understanding of the words, love, respect, honor, commitment and caring.

They are available (not married! Unattached!) To meet you and you them
both of you have compatible "normals."
They are specifically good looking example: tall, physically fit, blue eyes yada yada...
We are sexually compatible and enjoy each other's company
They are abundant in money

They are physically healthy, emotionally sound.
State if you would like this to be a lasting relationship. We
live and marry and stay together for the rest of our lives.
They are human (I'm just being funny- I hope this is a given
LOL)

> *Note- Remember, the Angels said, "You can't be
> someone's "good match, if you aren't theirs. This is
> equal energy exchange."
> *Additional note- Also know the *meanings* of the
> words you chose in the manifesting. It can make a
> huge difference in what you receive.

Manifesting a job

Take 3 long breaths in and 3 exhales out. Do this at your
own pace. Sit in a place you feel comfortable and peaceful,
indoors or outdoors.
Try to *feel* in your heart. Focus by holding your chest area
with both of your hands. Then know your body and mind
are now connected. You can state this aloud or within.
 Continue with your focus on asking equally for your new
opportunity.

If you need to stop and get a paper and pen to write or
add more details-please do this. Make your manifesting

accordingly.
Please use this outline:

I am and I allow myself to get hired at (plug in the name of the employer or type of job you desire here.) I will receive a fair contract. Both of us (employer/person) will be happy with the contract. I will honestly do the best job I can. I will be the best employee I can for (put company/employer). In return, the company pays me (put you amount you want fair and reasonable) amount of US dollars *or more.*

We (you and employer) are both happy and satisfied with the work I contribute. I am positive for the (company name or employer), myself and all of the company's customers (if any, depending on job)
I receive this job (insert a month and year) Earth dimension. We both help each other and respect each other in all aspect of business and work ethics. We have an equal energy exchange.

This asking for a job can be done very specific if needed. Write in a company's name you wish to work for, or boss' name to hire you.
If you have a specific field you are looking for you can word it towards that occupation.
If you want a job in another location, meaning another office, town, state, country, please fill that information in the appropriate area.
I feel you get the idea of this one!

Manifesting stuff

Take 3 long breaths in and 3 long exhales out. Do this at your own pace. Sit in a place you feel comfortable and peaceful, indoors or outdoors.
Try to *feel* in your heart. Focus by holding your chest area with both of your hands then know your body and mind are now connected.

Continue with your focus on asking equally your desired items.

You can state this aloud or within. If you need to stop and get a paper and pen to write or add more details-please do this. Make your manifesting accordingly.
Please use this outline:

I am and I allow myself to receive a <u>Bike</u> (add what you desire here). I will do my very best to take care of this bike the best I can, I will also exercise with it, appreciate it, and if needed lend it to a friend. For receiving this bike I will be grateful that I have the strength and opportunity to find, purchase or receive it and will express my gratitude appropriately. I deserve a bike. I will use it properly and be careful of others while I ride it. I receive this bike (add your month and year date here) Earth dimension.

Depending on what you are asking for you can make it equal in some way. You can see how inventive you can be when you desire something badly. Your wording will change due to the item you are asking to come to you. It is okay just keep the exchange positive.

Some people have been gifted, won or "found monies" to receive what they were asking appropriately for, that was how the items came to them.

Manifesting Knowledge & Self-realization

Take 3 long breaths in and 3 exhales out. Do this at your own pace. Sit in a place you feel comfortable and peaceful, indoors or outdoors.

Try to *feel* with your heart. Focus by holding your chest area with both of your hands. Then know your body and mind are now connected. Continue with your focus on asking equally for knowledge & self-realization.

You can state this aloud or within. If you need to stop and get a paper and pen to write or add more details-please do this. Make your manifesting accordingly.

Please use this outline:

I am and I allow myself to understand my mind and body. I would like to ask my higher self the all-knowing me, my soul to help me receive clarity and truly understand to collect knowledge of my human self (put here what you want information, clarity or knowledge of)

With this information, I will have self-realization of what I need to know in this lifetime to advance myself in all aspects of my life this year of ____(or a specific one, for example doing better at school or letting go of old negative relationships , prejudices, selfishness or being a victim of others taking advantage of your "niceness").

This knowledge will make me a better person. I will have self-love and I can treat others better when I understand myself. I can teach others about my experiences and how they might relate to them. I   want to have self-understanding as well as understanding others; I will look through other people's eyes or situations.

 I will also understand myself. I want to know more about my body and mind. I want and deserve to live happier. My knowledge is freedom; I can have it and share it with others. I receive this knowledge and self-realization <u>month and year</u> Earth dimension.

You may have something that happened to you in your lifetime that you want clarity about, this would be something you would plug in and ask about specifically.

"Humans sometimes hear us but they need to *realize* and *accept* the information."

Manifesting Money

Take 3 long breaths in and 3 long exhales out. Do this at your own pace. Sit in a place you feel comfortable and peaceful, indoors or outdoors.

Try to *feel* in your heart, focus by holding your chest area with your hands then know your body and mind are connected. You can state this aloud or within.

Continue with your focus on asking equally for manifesting money and abundance. Trust that money will come your way.

You can state this aloud or within. If you need to stop and get a paper and pen to write or add more details-please do this. Make your manifesting accordingly.
Please use this outline:

I am and I allow myself to create from me (these are options you can choose one or all) working for it, or by receiving or finding or acquiring large amounts of money of (Put a desired amount) _ or more. With this money I will take care of my responsibilities, I will live within my means. I will share and help others if needed.

I do this without wanting anything in return except a thank you (you must mean this part!) I can and I will bring money and abundance of opportunities to myself. I deserve this money to better my life and my family's life.

What energy I give out, I will receive without expecting. What is deserved will come my way (place your desired month and year date here) Earth dimension.

Other options and phrases you can add for manifesting money and abundance:
What I strive for will bring money my way from my work efforts.
Money can be new way of work or salary.
It could be winning an item and selling it for money.
I am open to receive money or values from the positive ways.
I will treat others as I like to be treated- and all abundance I am responsible for, in positive way.

Be well, Manifest Equal Energy always

The universes work in many ways. If you keep it positive, the return will be abundant whether it is money or lots of love.
The Angels want to share this last message to you all.

"Positive always breeds positive."

Be well, enjoy your new life of equal energy exchange and know you deserve goodness in your lives- share this knowledge with others.

"Every exchange is important; it reflects on the worlds-yours, ours, all energies of existence … we are all souls that live together."

Chapter 12

Success Stories

Every day I have been receiving letters of successes in reference to soul talking and manifesting. I chose to put these favorites in the book to share. The names of the successors have been changed for privacy.

Terry and James Soul talking success

Terry a 41 year old, single mother of 2, read this book and had an appointment with me discussing the energy exchange and soul talking technique. She wanted to make amends with the father of her children; she had felt anger and disgust. He never visited the children nor did he pay any child support.

Terry decided to release her soul of that negative energy for she wanted to feel light and love within and for her present life. Terry wrote out everything she wanted to say without blame and soul talked with James on the energetic level. She described her experience leveling out her emotions as beautiful. It was exactly 14 days later she heard a knock at her door and as she looked to see who it was, she felt chills up her arms and her total body. It was James at her door. James looked at her and smiled as he quickly handed her a check of 4 months child support and said he was sorry and quickly left her door.

Terry told me she almost fainted when she saw his face. She was flabbergasted that he handed her the check. She told me she imagined that in her soul talk to James he would bring "fairness."

Leslie and Jose the manifesting of a good match
Leslie a 68 year old widow was ready to have a relationship after 6 years of mourning her husband. She asserted the copy of the *manifesting a good match* I sent to my email list. Leslie took the time to write out what she wanted in a mate and what she could offer him. She put this all in writing.

She had no idea who this new man would be, but wrote it out and used her intention diligently as the directions were expressed in the email. Leslie set her intention to manifest this *new man.* She read her written notes and felt it would be true and they deserved each other. She did this once a week for 7 months. That 7 month mark was the month she met Jose. Of course she dated during the 7 months prior and had some dates. She said she learned about herself greatly- she felt as if a great new identity was born, the true Leslie.

3 months after meeting Jose age 74, he asked her to marry him. Leslie was ecstatic about the marriage proposal and all Jose's attributes.

Leslie visited me at my healing center to tell me her story. She shared how they met and how they were perfect for each other except for one small thing. I asked her what the small thing was. Was it something she could live with? Leslie explained to me that Jose wanted kids! Kids? I said. Yes, she replied. Jose wanted to adopt since he never had children. We looked at each other and said at the same time. *"At his age?"* He wants to have a new born?

 Leslie said, I don't think I can marry him with that intention. She said she had 2 grown children of her own and is a grandmother, but had no desire to have a new born at her age. She loves children but that was the one thing that could certainly be the deal breaker. We both laughed a bit and I asked her out of curiosity to show me what she wrote down as her manifesting guide. Leslie opened up her pocket book and took out the crumbled manifesting paper she wrote over 7 months ago. I carefully read each statement. I laughed as I saw that Leslie wrote "I want a family man." I laughed. I asked her what she meant when she wrote this statement.

 Leslie replied, I guess I meant it to mean someone who liked my family and I his? She told me she honestly just wrote that without true intention, but said those words every week.

We laughed some more and now knew where that expression "be careful for what you ask for, "came from- especially if you are manifesting a good match! She said she would start a new manifest- for Jose to be happy and fulfilled on his own and hoped he would enjoy her grandchildren as his own.

Two months later, Leslie called me to let me know Jose loved her grandkids as his own and fell off the bug of wanting to adopt at the age of 74! Wedding bells rang.

Dave the money manifesto

Dave a 32 year old single man was manifesting $4200 for an investment into a business. Dave wrote down his manifesting in detail; that he would earn that amount or more for his endeavor and would provide one person a job- other than himself from his investment of the $4200. Dave services pools for a living and wanted that money to build a stronger business.

I have to say Dave is one fast man-afesto! One month and one day later he received a call from a long time client that recommended him to 3 country clubs. They wanted a new pool company to service their pools on a weekly basis. Dave was the new guy. Guess what the dollar amount came to?

Dave now has a stronger business and hired one additional person to help him grow. He told me he worked hard and deserved the money. Dave also said he would help another person by hiring them to work with his new bigger company.

Soul talking Cindy

Cindy is a 28 year old beauty that had a pattern of allowing others to take advantage of her. The advantage in the means of having her pay for all dinners, movies, anything because Cindy had a hard time honoring herself and saying no. Cindy also was a person that was over giving in money and emotions. Cindy chose to allow herself to release all of these old patterns that made her life unequal and unfulfilling. She told me that she was never sure if her friends were truly her friends, since she offered and paid all the time for everything.

Cindy wrote down everything she wanted to release from her souls energy, this way she could move forward and allow herself to be assertive and loving at the same time with friends and people in general.

Cindy did the soul talking meditation 3 times over a period of 2 months before she knew and felt in her heart that she was done with that old thought pattern and old actions. She expressed that it took her time because *she* was the one who allowed feeling guilty instead of releasing it. She also shared that she did the soul talking technique with those "friends" that took advantage of her, because she allowed it. Cindy wanted all of them to be equal before she could move ahead.

The last time we spoke via email Cindy is super happy and hasn't had any negative or unequal exchanges since! Way to go Cindy!

Logan's self-Soul Talk- free of addiction

Logan a 22 year old was close to revisiting re-hab. He admits his addictive behavior for pharmaceutical drugs. Struggling, he came across the soul talking website. How? He still doesn't know. Logan said it just showed up on his computer! He took the time and truly wanted to change his ways. He soul talked 2 times with releasing his patterns of addiction with drugs and self-sabotage. So far he is 8 months clean and feeling great, has a new job and as quoted "my new life- *my* life is good and always better each day as I now decided to trust *me*."

Carrie surrendered to soul talking

 Carrie a 24 year old had low self-worth and had slept around with different men a lot. She called me to get advice on changing her habits. Carrie wanted to change herself to be happy. She said it was like a need to fill the void of her father not being around her as she grew up. I shared the empowerment skills of self-soul talking. I explained it was a form of self-healing on an energetic level. The information of how to cleanse and clear, then replace with positives to fill those voids became vivid to her.

She said she finally *"got it."* Carrie said at first it was hard for her to admit she wasn't acknowledged by her own father, but knew it was not anything she did. That is when she said she was ready to release all those negative thoughts and emotions. I was glad she understood the concepts. Carrie went forward and self-healed with soul talking. Each night she would write out why and who, then release. She worked on herself. Soul talking made her feel connected to her body and mind. 8 months later Carrie visited me in Florida, she had completely changed her perception of her father and her relationship with herself. She realized why, accepted it, and then let go of the self-destructive patterns in her life. Later that year she told me she chooses to be happy and that she honors and respects herself. Carrie also shared she is currently manifesting her good match!

Melanie and Kenny super match

Melanie 27, Kenny age 32 walked into my office for an appointment. Both sat on the blue comfy couch in front of me and Melanie said; I manifested him. I looked and smiled at them both. Then Kenny spoke "we are getting married this fall." Melanie and Kenny laughed as they told me that they wanted to thank me for sharing because Melanie apparently manifested Kenny within 6 months!

Try the Soul talking Technique or manifesting skills- Share your success! Email me your story.
Joliemfa@live.com   I'm tellin' ya- it ain't no jive!

Gratitude

I appreciate that you took the time to read this book, please gift it to another person. It's a positive energy exchange!

I gracefully thank my clients, friends and family; namely my mother. I send special thanks to Kathy McKay and all the wonderful Angel guides. Smiles☺

> "I *choose* & *allow* myself to live happily; I am the keeper of my soul."

About the author

  Jolie DeMarco is the "Messenger of the Light." She is a clairvoyant medium and community speaker. Jolie specializes in spiritual guidance, crystal energy healing and Light Tunnel energy. Jolie speaks of mindfulness and the energy exchange to large groups to educate and raise vibrations in communities. She is the proprietor of a Mindful Healing Center in Boca Raton Florida called My Flora Aura.

Jolie has written several books that might interest you, please explore. Available on Amazon or her website www.JolieDeMarco.com

Find Jolie on Facebook and YouTube –Jolie DeMarco channel.

"We come here knowing everything. Then we are de-programmed by other people, society, and living

conditions. Then we search our whole lives to find that knowing and contentment. We do this by re-programming ourselves into what we once were- that is pure light."

A wise soul once said;
'Like me for being a human. Forgive me for my opinions."

I shared the message with friends, we laughed as I explained the message came from *my* higher self.

Healing & Wellness Books

 Crystal –Mandalas and Mudras Self-Healing

 Stoned premium Crystal Grids for Healing & Wellness

 ## Oracle Deck

Self-Healing Mandalas- get a self-reading. Card decks purchase online available on **I-phone apps and android Google play**

 https://itunes.apple.com/us/app/mandala-card-reading/id581451501?mt=8

Jolie additionally wrote 3 Mindful Children's books ages 3-8.
They are available on my Amazon.

www.JolieDeMarco.com

To take a FREE 1 minute test to gauge how intuitive you
currently are. Go to: www.Getareadingnow.com

Try The New Soul Talking & Relationships oracle deck

Made in the USA
Las Vegas, NV
21 May 2021